The Will of God

The Will of God

Answering the Hard Questions

James C. Howell

WESTMINSTER
JOHN KNOX PRESS
LOUISVILLE · KENTUCKY

Unless otherwise indicated, Scripture quotations are from the New Revised Standard Version of the Bible, copyright © 1989 by the Division of Christian Education of the National Council of the Churches of Christ in the U.S.A., and are used by permission.

Scripture quotations marked RSV are from the Revised Standard Version of the Bible, copyright © 1946, 1952, 1971, and 1973 by the Division of Christian Education of the National Council of the Churches of Christ in the U.S.A., and are used by permission.

Book design by Sharon Adams
Cover design by Night & Day Design

First edition
Published by Westminster John Knox Press
Louisville, Kentucky

This book is printed on acid-free paper that meets the American National Standards Institute Z39.48 standard. ∞

PRINTED IN THE UNITED STATES OF AMERICA

09 10 11 12 13 14 15 16 17 18 — 10 9 8 7 6 5 4 3 2

Library of Congress Cataloging-in-Publication Data

Howell, James C.
    The will of God : answering the hard questions / James C. Howell.—1st ed.
       p. cm.
    ISBN 978-0-664-23290-0 (alk. paper)
    1. Provience and government of God—Christianity.   2. God—Will.   I. Title.
    BT135.H69   2009
    231'.7—dc22   2008022114

Contents

Preface

I have been trying to write this book for over twenty-five years. When I was a young man, I plunged into it with much zeal, but thought I should wait until I might become wiser. Unresolved questions nipped at my confidence, since a book on the will of God had better have all the answers, right?

Over these years, I have witnessed and personally experienced so much pain, loss, confusion, and darkness on the world stage, in my work as a pastor and in my own private life, that I know that it's time to say something. I hear constantly from people who just don't believe in God anymore, either because something terrible happened, or because life as a believer didn't seem significantly different from the life of everybody else. How many thousands of times have I heard little pithy sayings about God mouthed mindlessly, as if something you could print on a bumper sticker could be big enough to answer why we lose those we love the most? There are plenty of theological sound bites, loads of conventional wisdom, digestible morsels that cannot satisfy.

When the great hymn writer Isaac Watts was eighteen years old, he left a worship service and complained to his father about the deplorable singing and dreadful hymnody. His father said, "Well then, young man, why don't you give us something better to sing?" I have tried to write something that is better than the conventional wisdom, something humbler but more hopeful, closer to the heart of God.

This is not a theodicy, that valiant attempt among theologians to defend God's honor, to settle all questions in God's favor. Questions are not to be muzzled; God gave us questioning minds. How could any "answer" satisfy the storming questions we harbor after the death of a spouse, child, or friend? We will let our questions rise up. I do not pretend to have all the answers, but I do believe in this book you will find many true things, true to the character of God, true to life as we experience it.

For whom did I write this book? I have held in my mind cynics who think God simply cannot be, and friends who quit speaking with God some time ago. I have also hoped to speak with very religious people, for whom God's will seems so easy—and to provoke some discomfort. I have written with photographs on my desk of family and friends who have grieved heavily with me. I never let the horrors around the world drift out of my mind.

Whom should I thank? Probably every person who with superb intentions said something too trite to be true, those who have loved tenderly, simple folk who have followed Christ heroically, and also the hundreds I've visited in hospitals. I think of good-hearted people who could discover a richer dimension to life, and others who cannot locate any kind of compass to point their next steps. I remember a broad sea of faces, people I have buried, comforted, been quizzed by, worked alongside, prayed with, and loved deeply. Authors I have never met have transformed my thinking.

Then there are those special friends who have read my manuscript and bothered to tell me the truth, so the final product could be so much better: Jason Byassee, Sam Wells, Mark Ralls, Alyce McKenzie, Ben Witherington, Suzanne Putnam, Laurie Clark, David Burrell, and Lisa Stockton Howell. Don McKim and Jack Keller of Westminster John Knox were gracious in their encouragement to publish. They and so many others are faithful companions who help me to have some sense of God and hope in the face of bewilderment, delight, tears, and joy.

Introduction

Most theological questions I field from people have to do with one enormously important yet maddeningly elusive subject: the will of God. As it turns out, the will of God is not just one thing, but *two* things, although they are intimately related in surprising ways.

There is the question of *What is God's will for me?* What am I supposed to do with my life? What should I do in the next five minutes? If I knew clearly what God wanted, couldn't I at least get moving on it? Would it be something I could happily embrace? Or might it scare the daylights out of me?

Then there is a second question, which doesn't look forward to what I'm about to do, but instead looks back to something that happened, usually something awful. My husband was killed in a crash. The boss fired me. The tsunami destroyed thousands of lives. Cancer was diagnosed. My marriage dissolved. *Why do bad things happen?* Was my unspeakable loss God's will? Was God trying to tell me something? Why didn't God intervene? If God is good and has a plan, how do I make sense of suffering and evil? How many thousands of times have we muttered "Thy will be done"? What exactly have we been praying for? And what might the answer look like?

So we have two questions: *What does God want me to do?* and *Why do bad things happen?* At some moments in life, one question may feel more urgent than the other. But over a lifetime of bouncing from one question to the other, we discover the two questions are very close kin; the two become one. Perhaps we can answer *What does God want me to do?* more wisely because we have wrestled with *Why do bad things happen?*—and the more diligently we pursue what God wants us to do, the more we come to a deeper sense of why bad things happen.

The Mystery Made Known

It's hard to think of more important questions, for they cut right to the heart of the purpose and direction of my life. I want my life to make sense. Something in me resists the idea that my life is random, although it can feel that way. In the funny and emotionally profound movie *Forrest Gump*, Forrest stands over the grave of his young wife and muses, "Jenny, I don't know if Momma was right, or if it's Lieutenant Dan. I don't know if we each have a destiny, or if we're all just floatin' around accidental-like on a breeze, but I think, maybe it's both. Maybe both is happening at the same time."

Maybe we have a destiny, maybe we're just floating, maybe we are responsible, maybe God is orchestrating things, or maybe God leaves us largely to our own devices. How could we ever know?

I suspect that, when we explore questions about the will of God, we assume it's hard to decipher, that God has hidden this will, and I'm like a child poking my head behind bushes trying to find the little eggs God has tucked away with a message inside. While I am hunting, God is over on the sidelines, saying, "You're getting warmer!" or ". . . colder!"—or just not saying much at all.

In Bible times, the pagan religions were all about divination, seeking "signs" to figure out the divine will. Priests cut open animal cadavers and read livers, they unleashed birds and traced their pattern of flight, they studied the stars in their courses out in the dark. People were nervous all the time, fearful they had failed to figure out the whims of arbitrary, petty gods.

Israel, and then the writers of the New Testament, rejected all this. God "has made known to us the mystery of his will" (Eph.

1:9). Yes, God's will has a mysterious element—but God has made it known. In fact, God is bending over backward to make God's will known to us. God doesn't want us to lay out fleece or gaze about for signs, which are notoriously subjective. God wants a relationship. We don't need to master techniques to produce answers to our queries if we rely on a growing friendship with God.

We will never know God's mind fully. The glory of God resides in the humbling truth that God is magnificently large—staggering in scope and complexity—and our most brilliant theological thinking barely brushes the hem of God's garments. But we can know *enough* about what God wants us to do. And even when there is grey area and some confusion, we can still keep moving faithfully. We need not be baffled by wrecks, cancer, hurricanes, and all kinds of evil. We know *enough* to refuse to mistake God for a vengeful tyrant, even as we sit numbly in the dark and wonder why God seems to have vacated the premises. We can discover God's love in the thick of our darkest days.

The very effort to discover God's will is itself something God wills; the quest itself is fulfilling. To quit caring about God's will, to do whatever I wish, to decide there's no meaning out there is horror and madness. To pursue God's will, to insist there must be meaning, and to grapple with God until we get at least a hazy glimpse of it is happiness.

Questions Are Good

The will of God isn't the correct answer to a quiz that we flunk if we don't get it right. The will of God, for us, is a question—and questions are good! Sometimes we foolishly think faith is about having the answers. I hear people say, "I know I'm not supposed to question God; I am supposed to have faith." But faith is the raising of questions before God. Job, Jeremiah, and the psalmists voice hard questions to God. Jesus said, "Unless you . . . become like children you will never enter the kingdom" (Matt. 18:3). Children never stop asking questions, and they are under no illusion that they have all the answers. Faith is learning to ask all our questions, and even how to ask better questions.

To explore God's will, we never stop asking questions. But we also listen. Find someone who seems to live in sync with God, who exhibits a well-cultivated ability to do God's will, and then listen. Find someone who is suffering, don't avert your gaze, and then listen. In his chilling memoir of barely surviving the concentration camp, Elie Wiesel wrote of the "flames that consumed my faith forever," the "moments that murdered my God and my soul and turned my dreams to ashes."[1] To know God we go where faith may not survive, where God seems remote or as good as dead. What did Jesus cry out with his last breath? "My God, my God, why have you forsaken me?" (Matt. 27:46).

When we talk about God's will, people get upset, they disagree fiercely, they can't always think straight. The stakes are high, and generally speaking if people get engaged in conversation about the will of God, it is because they have personal stories. *Why do bad things happen?* is rarely a parlor game for intellectuals. When we hear someone question the will of God, we can bet it's someone who loved and then lost someone, who cannot shake the regret or dodge the shadows any longer.

If we grapple honestly and faithfully with the will of God, we will not emerge with simplistic, black-and-white tidbits of truth. In our culture of sound bites, instant messaging, and blogs, we may feel disappointed when the easy answers we thought would suffice flutter to the ground like dead leaves. While writing this book, I found myself on a radio show talking about the will of God. The host, not the friendliest interlocutor on matters of faith, posed a hard question just as the producer was gesticulating that the commercial break was rushing headlong our way: "How can you know what God wills? Give me an answer in three seconds." All I got out was something like "Uhhh . . ." and the ad jingle commenced.

I do not know God's mind on everything, but I do know that it is God's will that you cannot say anything meaningful about God's will in three seconds. Quick three-second sound bites about God are in plenteous supply, as are the blog-length little digests, and they misconstrue God's will every time.

We've all heard the bland truthiness plenty of spiritual people cling to as self-evident: "God is in control of everything," or "We cannot know why God caused that car accident," or "The door was open, so it must be God's will," or "God needed your spouse in heaven more than you did," or "It was his time to die"—a monotonous string of half-truths, half-baked, catchy but too trivial to bear truth. Once upon a time, when a great thinker paused for a good while before saying anything, you knew genuine wisdom was being formulated; now we scoff if a politician pauses for three seconds before blabbering a truthy sound bite. To speak truly of God, to move toward doing God's will, you pause, you stammer, you've barely started the "Uhhh . . ." and the ad is zinging away, but perhaps God's will was voiced in its failure to get a quick word in.

Still, we had better get *some* words in. Critics of Christianity have always browbeaten our faith precisely because of our seeming failure to solve the problem of God's will. The Church's first critics ridiculed a faith whose very founder suffered an ignominious fate, and in modern times best-selling books trash Christianity, claiming a good God cannot coexist with bad events. To despisers of the faith, atheism's clinching argument is the very existence of evil. The skeptics have good questions. But we *can* understand evil and suffering and believe even more deeply in God, even as we grieve losses, resist evil, and muster hope. If we probe the questions, we begin to notice that the God being dismissed isn't our God at all, but a straw man, a fiction that we have allowed to be fashioned in the public's mind because we who believe have settled for simplistic answers to mind-boggling questions.

But we can do better. We can know enough. . . .

Part 1

Chapter One

The God Who Wills

B efore we can say anything meaningful about the will of God, we have to ask, *Who is God?* and, *What is God like?* Sometimes we are tempted to say something or other about the will of God that frankly casts God as an unsavory brute, or as an iron-fisted despot, or as a conniving player of games. We need to say true things about God, and if we can divine who God really is, then we may as a natural reflex understand God's will.

In the intellectual climate in which we have been reared, much like the philosophical world in which Christianity was born, God is defined with lots of words with the prefixes *omni-, in-,* and *un-* : omniscient, omnipotent, infinite, ineffable, unchanging. But do a string of grand adjectives tell the deep truth about God? In their effort to safeguard God's greatness, do the *omni*s, *in*s and *un*s somehow throw a cloak over the heart of God? Does the Bible insist on so many expansive adjectives to explicate who God must be "by definition"?

The miracle of the Old and New Testaments seems to be that God is better than all the definitions. God is more like a story, a poem, an experience, intensely personal, breaking your heart and then thrilling your soul. Yes, God is all-powerful, but God's power is consumed with love—and not some wispy, flighty kind of love, but love that is solid, strong, courageous, sorrowful, hopeful, joyful, enduring.

The phrase "God's will" might feel like cold steel, an inflexible decree etched into time by a mighty potentate. But the will of the God of love is fraught with emotion. God is closer to me than my next breath, and God is determined to have a personal relationship with me. God loves me more than I love myself—and when you love, you will the good of the other person. You have desires for the one you love. You desire love from that person. You long for excellence in that person. God has wishes, God has a purpose, God makes choices, God is pleased (or displeased), God promises (and keeps promises), God delights, God grieves.

To know God's will, we must know God's heart. As shrouded in mystery and as occasionally baffling as God can be, we can know God's heart—and perhaps it would be helpful to think back into the recesses of time to weigh what is in God's heart.

When God Was Young

Let us go back to the beginning . . . or even *before* the beginning. Think back, far back in time, before your grandparents lived, before the great inventions of the modern world, before the Roman Empire, before the dinosaurs roamed the earth, before the big bang, or however it is you think the world came to be, before time itself, back when God was young.

God had a very important decision to make: "What kind of God am I going to be?" A perfectly understandable option would have been for God to settle on: "I'll just be God"—and no one would have questioned God. But this God felt in God's heart some urge to make something instead of dwelling in divine isolation, however splendid. That urge in God's heart to make something is the beginning of the will of God. God willed to make something.

As we now know, God made something that is so mind-boggling, so grandiose and yet delicate, so ridiculously massive and yet unfathomably tiny, that you could spend your lifetime trying to comprehend it—and you would never get your mind around one millionth of it. God cast the galaxies across the expanse of space, God made this earth with a stunning array of life and wonder. You cannot begin to take it all in.

God decided to make something—but that wasn't enough. As much as God delighted in constellations, nebulae, mountains, glaciers, forests, bacteria, orangutans, and wildflowers, God was lonely. Or so it seems: God wanted some creature with a peculiar affinity to God's own heart. Having made something as extraordinary as the universe, God then made us. A woman, a man, a child, more women, men, children, and finally you, me, us.

At this crucial knot in time, God had another important decision to make: "How will I connect with these creatures that I've made?" God had a number of options. God could have said, "I will fashion a network of strings, and attach them to the heads, hands, and feet of each person. I will control them like marionettes, manipulating them so they will always do my will. They will never do wrong. They will never hurt one another. My will never will be left undone." But God decided not to attach those strings to our heads, hands, and feet.

God could have said, "I will overwhelm them by my power. I will impress them with miracles repeatedly, I will make them tremble in awe so they dare not cross me. I will dazzle them with displays of my might, and guarantee that my will is done."

But God decided to do something more impressive. Instead of manipulating us, instead of overwhelming us, God decided to love us. What a terrible risk for God to take! If you have done any loving, you know your heart gets broken. God wanted to love, God was and is love, so God took the risk, knowing full well that God's heart would be broken. This was the most wonderful moment in the history of the universe: when God decided to love.

Looking back, we need not be surprised. God *is* love. God within God's essence has never been anything but love. God was love when God was simply God. God was a communion of love, and when God made everything that was made, it was nothing but love. Dante called it "the Love that moves the stars." Not to love would have been out of character for God. Manipulation and domination would have been impossible for God, since God is love.

When God was young, God courageously took on the risk of evil—and a hidden aspect of that risk was that God's own self would be shrouded, concealed behind the smoke of God's people behaving badly. God's true self would be questioned and even disbelieved when God's people couldn't see God out in the open, running the show smoothly. It seems that God understood what was at stake, and risked everything anyway.

Perhaps God even anticipated how marvelous it would be when we did notice the love of God in the thick of mystery and even peril, and how the virtues of an open world, with light and shadow, with freedom squandered and then graciously returned, with love's failure but then love's restoration, outweigh what any other world might be like. Yet even if we wish the universe were different, at the heart of literally everything is this: God decided to love.

Is God in Control?

Funny thing about love: Love can do many things, but love never controls. Believers ask, "Is God in control? Surely God is in control!" But God is love and, as Paul wrote so eloquently, love "does not insist on its own way" (1 Cor. 13:5). God has something God wants you to do, to be; God very passionately wants things to turn out a certain way, a good way. This is because God loves. A God who loves cannot pervert love by acting as a tyrannical megalomaniac who must have his way or heads will roll.

Is God in control? In a way, yes—long-term, eventually; big picture, yes. But day in and day out, no, God does not control things that happen, or you and me. At times I do God's will, but often I do not, and you don't either. God chooses not to determine everything; love does not insist on its own way. So we cannot simply conclude that whatever happens equals God's will. Lots of times God's will doesn't happen. Otherwise we wouldn't need to bother hunting down terrorists or criminals (unless we want to reward them for doing God's will). Otherwise we would simply go insane with rage against God every time a child dies.

If God loves more immensely than we can fathom, and yet if God does not insist on having God's way in every little thing, then God's heart is broken—all the time. Love "bears all things" (1 Cor. 13:7)—and we see this God of extraordinary grace grieving throughout the Bible, and throughout history. God waits, quietly, arms outstretched, pleading with us: "I was ready . . . to be found by those who did not seek me. I said, 'Here I am'" (Isa. 65:1). Instead of huffing and puffing and blowing our house down, God stands at the door and knocks (Rev. 3:20).

But to say that God does not control everything, to say that God is not a divine manipulator begins to feel as if we are saying God is remote, God is uninvolved, God doesn't care. Or else, God cares, but God is rather helpless, just standing by, shoulders slumped in exasperation on the sidelines when his team has just fumbled the game away. These feelings are understandable, palpable, and resonate in the aching heart. But God is far from uninvolved. God cares, more than you and I do.

God sees each one of us at every moment, with the intensity of a parent who looks up at the stage during a ballet recital: yes, there are two dozen ballerinas circling after an *échappé*, but the parent sees just one—my daughter, the love of my life. God, with extraordinarily focused panoramic vision, can pull this off for me, for you, for everybody else reading, those not reading, a few billion people simultaneously, not to mention my dog and the bird that just flew by my window. "His eye is on the sparrow, and I know He watches me," as the old hymn put it.

Is God like a Parent?

But shouldn't we feel a bit suspicious of this notion that God can be compared to a parent? Fond as many people may be of it, the idea of God-as-parent is riddled with difficulties. I cannot look at myself as an earthly father and say, "God must be like that." God isn't reducible to even the best humanity can muster. God is logarithmically beyond you and me on even our best days.

We cannot speak of God, as Karl Barth put it, by speaking of ourselves in a loud voice. God is so much greater, so unspeakably resplendent, so breathtakingly magnificent that our most cunning words, our most artistic painting, our most resounding symphony—the sum of all human genius—can only hint at a fraction of the wonder of God's being. God truly is omniscient, omnipotent, infinite, ineffable, omnipresent; God is so . . . well, words fail us, as even the *in-*, *un-*, and *omni-* words crumble under the weight of God's reality.

And yet, because God is all love before and after anything else, then God wants to be known, God wants a relationship, God wants to approach us and be approached by us. The way God does this is a mind-boggling surprise, and yet exactly what we would expect from a God who loves us. To understand God's will, we can look into our own hearts, into our own minds; we can listen to our own bodies. We see plenty there that is not of God; and yet God invites us to look and listen.

And why? God tries to connect with us down here, across the huge chasm between us and God. How does God do it? Genesis tells us that God made us "in the image of God." There is something in me that mirrors the mind and the heart of God. If I want to know the mind and the heart of God, I can look into my own mind and heart, and I can learn something there about God. God had to decide "What kind of God am I going to be?" You and I have to decide, all the time, "What kind of person am I going to be?" and so maybe from how we think about "What kind of person am I going to be?" or even "What is a parent like?" we can learn about how God decided to be one kind of God and not another.

I am a father. What kind of father will I be? Or, at this point, what kind of father have I been? The Apostles' Creed speaks of God as the "Father Almighty"; and we could just as viably think of God as the "Mother Almighty." But the one thing fathers (and mothers) like me down here on earth learn is that we are not almighty! I used to think I would be the kind of father who would shelter my children from all harm. What I have discovered is that the effort to shelter your children from all harm causes your children great harm.

I thought if I just hugged them enough, read to them every night, got them on the right team and with the right teacher, and if we did church, mission trips, prayer and Bible reading, they would turn out to be fantastic people—like following the recipe and baking a cake, perhaps? But then you discover that children are unique mysteries, and no formula can manufacture the person that fits your blueprint. They always surprise you, sometimes by breaking your heart, but other times by blossoming in some unimagined way.

I realize now I rather naively thought my children would always be with me, in my arms or holding my hand. But early on you hesitate but then relent, and you watch through tears as your child toddles off to day one of kindergarten, or you drive to a college campus and leave your child who's no longer a child at all, and it feels as if it's for good. Love lets the beloved child go, still loving, but letting go.

God really is a father, a mother to us. God gave us life, God loves. God is a spendthrift creator, not producing each of us as with a cookie cutter, or adding one by one as to a long line of toy soldiers. God weaves into each person's DNA some dazzling potential for us to turn out not just one way but a dizzying number of ways, and God enjoys watching, waiting, groaning, and then laughing. God scoots us out into the world, hoping we will pay regular visits back home, and read the letters God has written, and live in a way that makes the family proud.

God is well aware that it's dangerous out there. God made "out there"! But God decided: "I will not shelter them from all harm. What I will do is, I will love them; I will send my Son to be their brother. I will enter into their lives in such a powerful way that they can come to know my heart, so they can know my mind. And then they will know what I am calling them to do, and what my will for them is; and whenever they suffer, they can look to my Son."

We cannot forget for a moment that God is almighty in a way human mothers and fathers are not. But then what does the almightyness of God look like? We see God's might in God's Son; we know what we know about the will of God by looking to God's Son.

Jesus Is the Answer

One day this man named Jesus, who lived in the Middle East two thousand years ago, told his closest friends, "The one who sent me . . . is with me, for I always do what is pleasing to him" (John 8:29). You and I might fantasize about being able to say, "I *always* do what is pleasing" to God, but that would be fibbing. And yet we can still dream, can't we?

Sometimes we debate God's will, as if it is a memo God thought up just a few minutes ago. But to know God's will, we Christians need to go back in time and get as close as possible to Jesus. Or perhaps in our own time we have come to discover a sense of the risen Christ's presence. He is the ultimate embodiment of God's will: he exhibited God's will, spoke of it, fulfilled it. Jesus was, is, and always will be the will of God. God became flesh; so if you want to see God, start with your own heart, your own body—for we believe God took up residence in a body, with five senses, a heart, emotions, everything human in Jesus, who loved, laughed, desired, hungered, yearned, was disappointed, frustrated, and enraged, yet dreamed, wept, died, and finally leaped for joy.

Jesus is the answer to both our questions: *What does God want me to do?* and also, *Why do bad things happen?* as we will see. The more we know about Jesus, the more we focus on what Jesus did and said, on who he was (and is), the closer we will be to God's will, the more clarity we will have about God's will.

Not long before she died, Dorothy Day, one of the most stellar, down-to-earth, compelling Christians of the twentieth century, was asked to write some autobiographical reflections on her life. All she came up with was this:

> The other day I wrote down the words "a life remembered," and I was going to try to make a summary for myself, write what mattered most—but I couldn't do it. I just sat there and thought of our Lord, and His visit to us all those centuries ago, and I said to myself that my great luck was to have had Him on my mind for so long in my life![1]

We could shorten this book considerably and simply say, "Keep Jesus on your mind, and you will understand and do and be well within the will of God." Of course, we need the real Jesus, not one we fabricate to suit our personal preferences. Jesus spoke, and his words rattle our complacent spirituality and turn our comfortable lifestyles upside down; but didn't that voice from heaven say, "This is my Son, the Beloved . . . listen to him!" (Matt. 17:5)?

What did he say that could unveil God's will for us? "Do not store up . . . treasures on earth" (Matt. 6:19). "Love your enemies" (Matt. 5:44). And when you have a dinner party, do not invite those who can invite you in return, but "invite the poor, the crippled, the lame, and the blind" (Luke 14:13). We may wish Jesus had not said so much, or perhaps that he had said something different. His words shock, jostle us off balance—and the mystery of God's will is swept away into a cloud of flying dust every time we refuse him by saying, "Not *your* will, but *my* will be done."

Jesus was more action than talk, and we might mimic Jesus: we see him touching the untouchable or feeding the hungry, and we go and do likewise with the best motives we can muster, with the humble confidence that we are in God's will. We can even dare to go where Jesus' closest friends failed to go, to the cross. We see his holy, beautiful hands, side, and feet pierced. We see him forgive those who just perpetrated this evil against him. We hear him welcome a common criminal into paradise. We are moved by his tender care for his mother watching her son die a horrific death. And we feel a profound understanding of suffering, evil, love, and God's purpose building in our souls.

Jesus, too, had a choice to make. What kind of Son am I going to be? In recent years, those early gospels that didn't make it into the Bible have gotten a lot of attention. "The Infancy Gospel of Thomas," written perhaps more than one hundred years after our four Gospels, imagined Jesus trying to figure out what kind of kid he was going to be. A playmate poked fun at Jesus one day. Wielding not playground kid power, but divine power, Jesus waved his finger and struck the boy dead. Then, with the love of God rippling through his heart, he was filled with remorse. So he deployed that same power that struck the boy dead to raise him back to the land of the living. Jesus, in this legend, was trying to figure out, What kind of kid am I going to be?

Was Jesus' Death God's Will?

Jesus, perfectly mirroring God the Father, decided to be the kind of person who loves. The Gospel of John captures the essence of Jesus' heart: "Greater love has no man than this, that a man lay down his life for his friends" (John 15:13 RSV). Was the death of Jesus God's will?

For decades, Leslie Weatherhead's insightful book *The Will of God* has rightfully been a best seller. If I could correct one weakness in his book, it would be the way he thinks about the death of Jesus. He seems to say that God was trying other strategies to save us, but none of God's plans succeeded. So God thought, "I'll send my Son down, and maybe they will listen to him." But they didn't listen to him; they killed him. God didn't want him to be killed, but it happened, and God made the most of it.

I don't think that's right. The Bible's authors did not reduce Jesus to some "plan B" on God's part.

> Blessed be the God and Father of our Lord Jesus Christ . . . just as he chose us in Christ before the foundation of the world. (Eph. 1:3–4)

> He was destined before the foundation of the world, but was revealed at the end of the ages for your sake. (1 Pet. 1:20)

> In the beginning was the Word, and the Word was with God, and the Word was God. (John 1:1)

> He himself is before all things. . . . In him all the fullness of God was pleased to dwell. (Col. 1:17, 19)

I think that before God made the first star, God made up God's mind to make the world and to make us in the world, and God decided we would be mortal—knowing hearts would be broken. And yet God knew that this was the only way that we would really treasure life and appreciate the glory of eternal life, and love itself.

So when God decided to make us mortal, God at that same moment decided that "Mortality is so bad, death is so painful, that I will let my own heart be shattered; I will send my own Son. The world will unleash its fury on him—or really on us. He will suffer a terrible, unjust, untimely death, when he is too young. And when that happens people will know that I understand their pain and anguish from the inside. But I won't leave my Son dead in that grave. I will raise him up so that the people that I will have made and that I will love so much will trust me, and always have hope." God decided that before God did anything else.

Jesus is the power of God. But Jesus was not an arbitrary show-off, like Bruce Almighty, the film character who was temporarily granted divine powers—and sophomorically burst about doing what you and I might do were we all-powerful. Jesus was humble, meek, merciful. Christmas celebrates the truth that the power of the entire universe was focused into a very small bundle of an infant crying in the dark in Bethlehem. Lent disciplines us as we walk for forty days with this Jesus who did not turn stones into bread even when he was hungry. In Holy Week we follow the children's band, waving palm branches, puzzled but mesmerized by the love of this humble Savior who governed the world by standing silent before a fake governor, Pontius Pilate. He didn't explain evil, he didn't crush evil; he bore evil, he triumphed over evil, but in a hidden, proleptic way.

Jesus didn't thump his enemies, or call down thunder on those who imitated him badly. He was merciful, open, receptive; his love was resistible, and evil crossed him in cruel ways. So in Jesus we see that God's will isn't an ironclad steamroller. You need not fear a mistake or two (or a thousand): God's will isn't a long railroad track, where if you get derailed you are unsalvageable wreckage. Jesus joined hands with people who had lost their way, and loved them, stuck with them, died for them, and didn't linger in the tomb for long. God's will is like that.

But to many of us today, Jesus strikes us as a once-upon-a-time wax figure in the museum of religious relics. Can Jesus help in the complexities of today's world? Between the Internet, globalization, terrorism, the march of science, and the nihilistic lure of our consumer culture, is it really as simple as merely keeping Jesus on my mind?

The Holy Spirit

Jesus anticipated his own absence from the world scene, which perfectly mirrored the way God had always been very present but not in your face. On the night before he died, he unveiled the steady tenderness in the heart of God: "I will not leave you desolate" (John 14:18 RSV). Here's the plot: God the Creator made everything when time began. Then, in the fullness of time, God sent his Son, Jesus, who was in some way God incarnate, the Word made flesh. But when he left, when his earthly term was finished, he pointed to yet another, a third person within God, the lingering presence of God: the Holy Spirit.

Within the broad spectrum of Christendom, there seem to be two kinds of people: there are those who are very confident about the Holy Spirit, what the Spirit has just said, what the Spirit is urging, how the Spirit is empowering me right now; and then there are also those who are puzzled by the whole idea of the Spirit, are uncertain of the Spirit's movements, and frankly do not know what to say (if anything) about this mysterious third person of the Trinity. These two groups drive each other to distraction, and when it comes to the will of God, both are right in a way, and both come up short in another way.

There is a Holy Spirit. God loves so much that God never leaves us alone. In worship, the Spirit moves, teaches, heals. Every breath you take is the Spirit's gracious labor over your life. All insights, every recognition of theological nonsense, the motivation to holy actions are all the Spirit's relentless activity. Without the Spirit, we quite literally don't have a prayer of knowing or doing the will of God.

And yet, the Spirit is elusive. Even the most brilliant Christian artists, who have painted the Creator and sculpted Jesus so magnificently, have faltered with the Holy Spirit. Frederick Dale Bruner called the Spirit the "shy" member of the Trinity, as if the Spirit prefers anonymity, as if the Spirit's true joy is like the guy on the lighting crew or the woman who supplies costumes for the actors out on stage, preferring the spotlight to fall on others. The Spirit is demure, preferring our focus to be on God the Father, on God the Son.

This habit of the Spirit, to lurk in obscurity, to make things happen without demanding credit, tells us something crucial about the heart of God. If we want to know and do God's will, if we want to make sense out of suffering and why evil tramples the good, we have to acknowledge at the outset that there is something in the heart of God that will be forever backstage, out of the bright lights. God is elusive, God is there but hidden in shadows, God acts in ways we cannot see or fully understand. There is an anonymity about God's involvement in the world. If someone trumpets crystalline clarity about God's will, that person hasn't come to know the shy member of the Trinity.

What God Has Already Willed

And yet if someone shrugs and despondently announces that we just can't know much about God's will, then that person also hasn't come to know this shy member, who wants us to know about God and fulfill God's will more than we do. This is in God's heart: for us to know *enough* about God and God's will.

In the Introduction, we highlighted these words: "[God] has made known to us the mystery of his will" (Eph. 1:9). Now let us extend that a bit with more wisdom from Paul: "Ever since the creation of the world [God's] invisible nature . . . has been clearly perceived in the things that have been made" (Rom. 1:20, RSV). What is the largest, most illuminating textbook in our course on the will of God? Just look around. If you want to know what God wills, consider what God has *already* willed, and from that we can pick up on patterns in God's heart, the habits of God's desires.

Look at the world, God's masterwork. Don't let the view get blocked by all the phony man-made stuff—which might be evidence of God's will, but just might be human chicanery. Look at the beauty of creation, the expanse of the galaxies, the delicate petal of a rose, the clouds gathering, the scampering of a chipmunk, the face of your grandmother, or the fingers of an infant. Feel the warmth of the sun or the breeze at your back, hear the boom of thunder or the crickets chirping in the dark.

God willed it, God sustains it, God keeps the loving promise to the universe and to us who depend on God "in whom we live and move and have our being." God made everything, and called it "good," although this goodness can be tricky for us to perceive. We see what we think is good, but it's a faked good in a fallen world, and we fail to see the true good because our vision has been blurred.

In some church traditions, Christians greet one another by saying, "God is good." And how do you respond? "All the time." In my unscientific poll, those most likely to indulge in this litany of greeting are the poor, those living in challenging circumstances. Try saying, "God is good" to rich, comfortable, educated people. Most will squint a little, pause, and then engage you in some banter about when they think God is good and when they kind of wonder. Travel the world, and you find Christians in exceedingly poor regions, in Africa, South America, and Asia, who are buoyant with a rich awareness of God's goodness. They are swift to acknowledge: "God is good, all the time."

God is good all the time, not just occasionally or in special circumstances. We think too narrowly about the notion of God's "intervention," as if God is generally uninvolved—but then suddenly God dips a divine finger into the course of events. God is not a distant relative who pops in occasionally with a gift; God doesn't need to show up, because God is already there.

If we cut to the heart of things, nothing is merely "secular" as opposed to "sacred." God made it all, God is in the laws of gravity and photosynthesis, the breaths you take as you read and the stars tracing their courses across the sky. We have thrown mud on the sacred, and twisted it into contorted shapes. But like an old coin, no matter how scratched, faded, or tarnished, even if it has been run over by a train, the image is indelible, the sacred is everywhere.

Creation teaches us that God wills beauty, and that God is delighted when your jaw drops over some wonder you hadn't noticed a minute ago. God made the world so big that you can never see it all; yet earth itself is barely a grain of sand on the vast seashore of the universe which borders on—what? God? God's purpose is big, really large, hugely enormous, never to be reduced to me and my petty agenda.

During the agony of the Civil War, Abraham Lincoln spoke to combatants, Yankees and Rebels, the blue and the grey: "Both read the same Bible, and pray to the same God; each invokes His aid against the other. . . . The prayers of both could not be answered. . . . The Almighty has His own purposes."[2] What did God say through the prophet of old?

> My thoughts are not your thoughts,
>   nor are your ways my ways, says the LORD.
> For as the heavens are higher than the earth,
>   so are my ways higher than your ways,
>   and my thoughts than your thoughts.
>   Isa. 55:8–9

This world cannot be mastered. For all our wizardry and technology, the wind and sea are too powerful to submit to the human enterprise. For all our brilliance in medicine, people we love still get sick and die, and they always will.

So God's will isn't for me to be able to manage my little world to my satisfaction; God isn't a tech-help, fix-it assistant I summon and then send back home when what's broken works again. God's will isn't total security, health, and happiness. God made the world with an edge, with some peril built in. Dante spoke of "the Love that moves the stars," but love never guarantees smooth sailing. If you love, you laugh, but you also weep, and when we probe the hidden plot of the world God has willed, we find both delight and agony. Evidently this is God's will.

If God loves, then this world and our life in it are about the drama of love offered, love blossoming, love missed, love refused, love relentless, love finally noticed, love ultimately returned, love consummated. Love thrills, and love hurts. In *Evil and the God of Love*, John Hick tried to explain why God would make such a world:

If there is any true analogy between God's purpose for his human creatures, and the purpose of loving and wise parents for their children, we have to recognize that the presence of pleasure and the absence of pain cannot be the supreme and overriding end for which the world exists. Rather, this world must be a place of soul-making. And its value is to be judged, not primarily by the quantity of pleasure and pain occurring in it at any particular moment, but by its fitness for its primary purpose, the purpose of soul-making.[3]

God's Will Is a Relationship

God's purpose, we hope, is far more than merely the making of souls. But since we have begun with who God is, we can explore the will of God having banished the bad idea that God is capricious, or a stern rule enforcer. God is personal, God is love; we know beyond any shadow of doubt that God wills a relationship with us. God is rouseable, as in Jesus' story about the friend banging on the door at midnight for some bread (Luke 11:5–8). If we apprehend God's will, it is not through intellectual banter, but by prayer, that expression of love that unites us by the Spirit with Jesus.

So let us pray these words St. Francis encouraged his friends to pray:

> Almighty, eternal, just and merciful God,
> grant to us . . . the grace to do for you
> what we know you want us to do.
> Give us always the desire to please you.
> Inwardly cleansed, interiorly illumined
> and enflamed with the fire of the Holy Spirit,
> may we be able to follow in the footprints
> of your beloved Son, our Lord Jesus Christ.[4]

Continuing prayerfully, we turn now to explore the question *What does God want me to do?* We might admit that we feel a little bit impatient. If you are reading a book called *The Will of God*, you may feel an urge to thumb ahead to the later chapters to get on with the big question of *Why do bad things happen?* Feel free to do so. And yet I believe we are unlikely to make much sense out of the question *Why do bad things happen?* if we haven't invested our lives in answering (and then getting busy with) the question *What does God want me to do?*

At one level, lots of bad things happen because people don't do what God wants them to do, whether I bring suffering on myself, or the horrid decision making of somebody else brings suffering on me—or if *my* horrid decision making brings suffering on somebody else! Why do bad things happen? The answer often is another question: Why do we sin as we do and cause so many bad things to happen? Or, Why do we refrain from the good when we could stop bad things from happening?

But there is more. To grasp the logic of why things happen, to have a feel for the way God acts (or doesn't seem to act) in the world, we need to be the kind of people who think about God all the time, trying to do what God wants, sensing God's presence, God's direction, God's patience in the things we do day to day. And, if we are more practiced at doing God's will, and if we are more familiar with the heart of God, we're better prepared to weather the bad things that happen—not to mention the fact that we're also better prepared to help others who suffer when their bad things happen.

So, let us together begin to explore the first of our twin questions regarding the will of God. What does God want me to do?

Questions for Discussion

1. In what ways are you conscious of doing God's will? of not doing God's will?
2. How is it helpful to see Jesus as the embodiment of the will of God?
3. How can we practice the will of God in our daily lives?

Chapter Two

God's Will for Me

W hat does God want me to do? How would I know such a thing? To many of us, the question feels mystifying. We wish God would just shoot us an e-mail or a memo; a whisper in the ear might do the trick. If God has something God wants me to do, God really ought to be more forthcoming with directions. If I don't do God's will, can't I just plead ignorance?

But then we all know people for whom God's will seems utterly clear. A few years ago, a couple beaming with excitement exited worship and said to me, "While you were preaching, we saw the Holy Spirit on the back of your head." I assured them that it was my grey hair, a bit more luminescent than usual from the late morning light filtered through the stained glass behind me. But they went on to say, "The Holy Spirit" (from the top of your head) "told us that it is God's will for us to move to Colorado." I tried to reckon whether this was good news or not.

So many people think of God's will this way. Somebody's grey head, the lights flicker, a chance occurrence, the door was open, a curious coincidence: a "sign." Bruce Waltke, in his very fine book on God's will, called this the "Hunch Method." You have some kind of hunch. You're looking for some kind of sign, and then it becomes . . . God's will. Fond as many religious people are of this method, we have to admit that Waltke is right when he concludes,

"Too many people have used the 'hunch' method to rationalize poor decisions or excuse their carnal living."[1]

Isn't it usually something like "We were driving down the street, and at precisely that moment a realtor was hammering a 'For Sale' sign in the yard of the dream house we'd always wanted; how cool that God let us know it was time to move"? Or "The morning after we read about Jesus saying, 'Follow me' in Bible study, my boss called me in to offer me a promotion to move to San Diego"? Why don't we ever hear people say, "I was walking downtown, saw a beggar, and knew God was calling me to leave my law practice and become a missionary to the Sudan"? Or "I was playing poker, was dealt the three of hearts, and figured God was telling us to take three abandoned children into our home"?

A hunch about God's will might by sheer luck coincide with God's will, but can't we do better? Does God speak only to the intuitive? Can't we admit we look for signs that work to our benefit and ignore any that might demand serious sacrifice? Should we rely on quirky spiritual happenstances, or instead rely on our closeness to God? Leslie Weatherhead wisely suggested that "The greatest help available in discerning the will of God is reached when we deepen our friendship with him."[2]

The good news is that such a friendship is possible! To me, when thinking about what God wants us to do, we return once more to Ephesians 1:8–9 (RSV): "[God] has made known to us in all wisdom and insight the mystery of his will." God's will is a mystery, indeed. But God has made known that mystery. God has provided tantalizing, powerful hints of who we are to be, how we are to live. God wants you to know God's will. In fact, God is far more eager to tell you God's will than you are to figure it out.

Can we know God's will with impeccable clarity? Of course not. But we can know *enough*. God has told us enough so we can live out God's will. You and I will never become masters who have God's desires accurately mapped out. But God has given us enough; God will always give us enough. How hopeful! Like a mother loving her son, like a husband wanting to know his wife's heart, like the laborer doing his best, like the artist striving toward something envisioned in the heart, we never love or work or know as fully and flawlessly as we might like. But it can be enough.

The Script We Follow

How do we know enough of God's will? If signs and hunches are unreliable, where do I find this will of God? "Your word is a lamp to my feet and a light to my path" (Ps. 119:105). The lens through which I understand what God wants me to do, what God has already willed, and what God is about to will—in the world, and in my life—is the Bible. We get too hung up on whether to take this or that item in the Bible literally, and we forget that the Bible is something God wanted to happen, and God's desire is that we read, listen, immerse ourselves in it, and view everything in our lives from its perspective. The Bible is our script, stage directions for players performing God's will.

To cynics, this "Bible answer" might sound corny. We can understand the ways Bible reading is hard, and how it has brought us up empty more than once. But God's will is there; it really is. Why phone up God with some appeal ("God, tell me what your will is on this major decision?") when we haven't patterned our lives today, yesterday, and last year on what God has willed to put right in front of us all along?

People who are deeply involved with God via Scripture don't agonize so much over God's will, because they are "in shape" spiritually, they sense the grammar, they have strong footings on which their quest for God's will is constructed. So you can start planning now to figure out what God's will might be next year or in twenty-five years: become a student of Scripture.

To people flailing over seemingly basic decisions, I am tempted to say, "If you just had a passing familiarity with the basics of the Bible, you could resolve this easily." There is so much that is so clear, so simple, so doable, in the Bible. You could spend your entire lifetime keeping busy with what you could be absolutely positive *is* God's will. "Do not get drunk" (Eph. 5:18), "Do not judge" (Luke 6:37); and we're told to "care for orphans" and "keep oneself unstained by the world" (Jas. 1:27); "The fruit of the Spirit is love, joy, peace, patience, kindness, generosity, faithfulness, gentleness, and self-control" (Gal. 5:22–23). It is God's will that we be holy, lift up the poor, reconcile with enemies, avoid gossip, keep promises, attend worship, clothe the naked, and express gratitude.

Reminding myself of this demystifies God's will for me, and frankly makes it feel more comprehensive—and daunting!—than merely waiting until a crisis and thinking, "Now I need to know God's will." For knowing God's will is a matter of developing holy habits. Over years of reading the Bible, we find God has used its many words to craft within us a mentality that mirrors Christ; we learn to act faithfully, and to think theologically in the face of tragedy. God is a God who makes and keeps promises, and so God's will is trustworthy long-term, able to weather any storm. God owns everything, so it is never God's will for me to be possessive or grasping. God sacrificed his Son, so God's will probably involves my making sacrifices. If you notice gifts in you (Are you smart? good with numbers? Do you cry when children suffer? Is there money in your pocket?), their proper use is for the glory of God, not your personal advancement. The more I practice what I know is God's will, the better prepared I am to improvise in a sticky, less-than-clear situation.

Improvise? Indeed. We have to grapple with the fact that every day we have decisions to make, but there don't seem to be handy Bible passages that help us get a handle on what to do. Is God silent on such matters? Or is some creativity required? Sam Wells suggests that the Christian life is a kind of "improvisation."[3] Well-trained actors learn their characters so well that they can cope when an entrance is botched or someone forgets the lines; you know your character, you stay in character. You improvise together with others on stage, not being original or innovative, but consistent, faithful to the story.

God does not seem to have supplied us with complete instructions for what to do this afternoon or tomorrow. We have to improvise—but not randomly! We can live out what is *un*scripted because we know what *has* been scripted. The Bible is a training school; our regular worship is a rehearsal. Christians make mistakes! But like actors in rehearsal, the mistakes become opportunities to learn, to grow, to improve.

Too much of our praying happens when we are in dire straits. Too often we think of Christian ethics as making a hard decision in a crisis. But our goal is to be near Jesus all the time, so that being about God's will is as normal and as constant as breathing. Wells is right: "Ethics is not about being clever in a crisis but about forming a character that does not realize it has been in a crisis until the 'crisis' is over."[4]

Much of the will of God is clear. But for the rest, that is less obvious: How will we know and then do God's will? We don't know just yet. So we will study the script, learn our parts, and then improvise, and in a way that will strike onlookers as fitting, given the beginning of the drama, given the way God has acted in history, given the life, teaching, death, and resurrection of Jesus, given the great examples of saints who have gone before us. Despite our foibles and sin, God trusts us, and gives us immense responsibility. "Response-ability": God has made us *able* to *respond* to God's grace.

So we do what we know is God's will: We listen to Scripture, sing hymns, pray, discuss, give money, serve at the shelter, knowing that we are being shaped to respond appropriately, faithfully, courageously to the grace of God—and that wherever we find ourselves on the stage of life, in that place God will be loved, and the will of God will be done.

Testing God's Will

So I'm about to do what I think is God's will—but is it really God's will? Or, I just did what I thought was God's will—but was it really God's will? Early Christians were warned: "Do not believe every spirit, but test the spirits to see whether they are from God" (1 John 4:1). In a way, we are freed from fretting too much about this: the very desire to please God pleases God. And we know that doing God's will is like a toddler getting his legs under him: you wobble and bang your head a lot.

Sometimes we latch onto bogus indicators. We think: "If it was God's will, then it should have succeeded marvelously." But sometimes God's will yields no obvious results. We follow God in hope—hope being that dogged determination to do what is right and good whether it stands a decent chance of working out successfully or not. Often things succeed splendidly—but God wanted something else. What God calls us to frequently plunges us into what feels like failure or suffering. How well did things turn out for Jesus at Calvary? or for the martyrs? or even for you the last time you took a stand for God and somebody sneered?

Extremely dubious is what I call the "open door fallacy." Someone says, "The door opened, so it must be God's will." But there are many open doors through which you most certainly should not walk; while sometimes to do God's will you bang on a closed door repeatedly until you crash through. The promotion to San Diego is an open door, but then so is the person willing to have an extramarital affair with you. Don't take the open door. During the early days of the civil rights movement, America said, "No," but citizens kept marching and had jail doors slammed behind them. Trying to find housing for the homeless mother who wandered into your church seems impossible, or you feel trapped in a job that demands you compromise your faith. Take the closed door—break the thing down if you have to.

If I am doing God's will, then will I find myself busier than ever? and tireder than ever? God's will isn't necessarily a whopping increase in doing, for the devil "often tries to make us attempt and start many projects so that we will be overwhelmed with too many tasks, and therefore achieve nothing," as St. Francis de Sales[5] taught us. Just before Jesus said, "Take my yoke upon you," he offered a tender invitation: "Come to me, all you that are weary and are carrying heavy burdens, and I will give you rest" (Matt. 11:28). Not "I will give you even more to do," and not "I will really wear you out." God's will involves those bizarre habits portrayed in the Bible, like observing the Sabbath day, or the liberating request from a loving God: "Be still, and know that I am God!" (Ps. 46:10).

Some say doing God's will brings peace to your soul. Indeed, we never know peace until we get in sync with God's will. But doing God's will isn't the end to all your problems, the absence of conflict, smooth sailing, or an easy chair. In fact, if we do God's will we introduce a whole new set of problems, challenges, and difficulties into our lives! Serving God is hard—which is a clue to why it is meaningful.

Beyond any question, God's will isn't measured by good feelings and sunny results. Doing God's will may bring suffering in its wake. No—doing God's will absolutely *will* bring suffering. Jesus did God's will, and suffered, as did all his disciples, and countless Christians through history. Prison cells and crosses were common destinations for Jesus' first followers.

Mother Teresa spoke of "love in action":

> You must give what will cost you something . . . giving not just what you can live without but what you can't live without or don't want to live without, something you really like. Then your gift becomes a sacrifice, which will have value before God.[6]

Perhaps we don't grasp the will of God because we cling so tightly to what we think is ours; we want to give what is convenient instead of what is costly, and so unwittingly we insulate ourselves from the will of God. Only when we feel that ache of yielding something precious do we embrace God's will for us. In a world that vaunts itself arrogantly against the grain of God's goodness, why would it even be conceivable to do God's will and not clash with the world and wind up taking a drubbing or two?

What about when I look back with regret? I tried to do God's will but I failed miserably. The inability to do God's will isn't evil. God's will forever exceeds our reach, so we keep striving, we never get puffed up with pride, and we glorify God who can be glorified even in our infirmities: God's grace "is made perfect in weakness" (2 Cor. 12:9).

God's Plan for My Life

If we think about God's will as a "script," we have to be careful to resist our understandable tendency to strain to see too far down the road, to thumb ahead to the end of the book to see how things turn out. With great eloquence, Leslie Weatherhead explained our problem:

Sometimes I have made a mistake myself by trying to discern the will of God for years ahead. I have come to the conclusion that God does not encourage us to see too far ahead. One simply must accept the fact that one has no idea where the road one is treading is going to lead. Suffice it to say that when one gets to the crossroads one will know which way to turn, and although we like to think that it is terribly important not to make a mistake—and I repeat one can never be certain that one has not made a mistake. . . . Our mistakes, if made in good faith, will not result in our being lost.[7]

After all, God's will is a relationship. If I spend a day in the Appalachian Mountains with my wife, I am not sure whether she will want to hike a trail on the Blue Ridge Parkway or stop off at the Folk Art Center. But I never get lost. I just stick near her. What is the script? The thrill is in not being so certain. We go here now, and I trust her with wherever we wind up next.

So it is with God. What is faith? Knowing and agreeing to everything in advance? Maggie Ross spoke of faith as "a willingness for whatever."[8] One of my most precious treasures is a handwritten note someone secured for me from Mother Teresa. What did she write? "Let God use you without consulting you."

God called Abraham: "Go from your country . . . to the land that I will show you" (Gen. 12:1). Which land might that be? God did not show him just yet. Jesus walked up to some fishermen and out of the blue told them to put down their nets and "Follow me" (Matt. 4:19–20). Where? They did not know yet. But they went wherever Jesus went; their path was defined not by destination, but by proximity to Jesus, who kept moving around.

Where will God lead you and me? We do now know yet. Faith is risky: we leave the cocoon of our preplanned, carefully managed lives and go—where? We do not know yet. Wherever God leads, that is where we will go. But we know whom we are following, and we want to be near him, and that is enough, for he is the fullness of life—he is the way, the truth, and the life.

What is God's plan for my life? is a question we cannot help asking. But the Bible simply doesn't talk about such a thing as

"God's plan for my life." In Jesus' day, people ground out a living in backbreaking toil, falling asleep exhausted at the end of the day, only to get up the next morning and work all day, hoping it would rain so something would grow and the family could have a few bites to eat. People then didn't think through a romantic plot for all of life. Today was what mattered. And it was on one of those todays that Jesus told the fisherman to put down their nets and follow him. Where? He did not tell them. If he had, they probably wouldn't have followed! But they went, one step at a time, one day at a time. *One moment*

Think of the ancient psalmist who wrote that God's word is a "lamp to my feet" (Ps. 119:105). How far ahead can you see with a lantern—and a Bronze Age lantern at that, not one of those brilliant outdoor beacons people use today? Not far. But far enough. You see well enough to take the next step, and the next step. The end of the road is all darkness. But it will be lit when you get near enough.

So along the way, you have to do some trusting. Each step is a step of faith. What, after all, is this "lamp to my feet"? God's word. How much light is there in a word? Can you see a word? Words are not solid—they shed no real light—but they are what we need on the journey. The psalmist, I think, imagines God speaking gently to us, over and over: "Here, this way, ooh, watch out, good job, over here, step up, keep coming, stop for a minute, rest awhile, get moving now, hurry through here . . ." The invisible word becomes the sure light.

How do we hear this word? God speaks, and God speaks primarily through the Bible, and we familiarize ourselves with the cadence and accent of God's voice by hearing it over and over, reading, studying, reflecting with others. Then, on that dark night, and even in the broad light of day, God guides us as we move forward, telling us only what we need to know right now, for the very next step. God's will is a mystery, a mystery made known, but a mystery.

If we know God's will, it is not ultimately because our technique, our Bible reading, or our praying wrested a nugget of guidance from God's hand. God's will is a gift. We receive it with open hands, stunned to be given something so precious, knowing we could never in a million years have figured this out for ourselves.

The Quakers (not surprisingly, since their worship is about listening in silence instead of directing a lot of racket toward God) have understood the discernment of God's will in ways that are helpful.[9] We take time, we listen, we wait, we test, we listen some more, we converse, we wait some more, knowing that ultimately discernment is the gift of God's Spirit. What the Quakers are especially vigilant about is the intrusion of "self" into the effort to hear God, the nagging persistence of sin even in spiritual veterans. While the next section of this chapter will feel less sunny than where we've been so far, it is as important. For until we confess our inability to know God's will, and in fact until we expose our ferocious resistance to God's will, we have no chance to hear, much less do, what God wants for us.

Questions for Discussion

1. Why do you suppose God has not revealed the complete divine will to us, but only "enough"?
2. What parts of God's will are "clear" to us? What parts are "less obvious"?
3. Have you ever tested God's will? What were the results?

Chapter Three

God's Will Undone

I wish doing God's will were as simple as just praying, reading the Bible, garnering our commission, and then simply acting on it. But the reality is as if we are baking a cake, and in a fit of madness we throw in too many eggs or even some arsenic, or we forget to take the thing out of the oven. We fail, we self-destruct, we just plain refuse God. We botch God's will all the time.

However, we don't feel like lawless rebels all that often; we don't seem like wicked people. But we just let our hearing go bad over time, we get too busy to listen; we hear what we want to hear, and selectively we become deaf to much of what God is telling us. We baptize our own little biases and pretend they are of God.

Most haunting of all, even if I know and really am determined to do God's will, the sober, humbling truth is that I am simply not able to. Sometimes I get it done, but then much of the time my inability to do God's will makes me blush. And it's not mere failure. I succeed, rather perversely, at doing things I know very well are not God's will and, sad to admit, I secretly relish my rebellion.

When I look inside my soul, unless I am brainwashed by some misguided self-righteousness, I find in myself what T. S. Eliot aptly called "shabby equipment." We must cope with the fact of sin if we want to know God's will. If we try to do God's will, we battle upstream, for we strive in a world that theologians describe as "fallen." God willed the universe, and you and me, into being. God made everything good; but we twist and ruin it; we want to *be* God instead of letting God be God. We mimic Adam and Eve, and find ourselves outside the garden God intended for us (Gen. 3).

The world's great beauty is muddied. The glory of the human body is perverted into something tawdry; brilliant minds hack into computers instead of curing cancer; lovely species are snuffed out by machinery belching smoke. Since Cain and Abel, brothers, and then nations, find reasons to stomp on and kill each other instead of befriending and helping each other.

The flawedness isn't just out there: it's in me, in all of us. Dark impulses cloud our souls, and even when we strive to do good we exhibit a creepy self-righteousness. No self-help program can cure the soul's malady. In the musical *Camelot*, Lancelot du Lac boasts of his physical and moral prowess, singing "Had I been made the partner of Eve, we'd be in Eden still." But Lancelot's ethical arrogance was exposed when he had his affair with Guinevere. Had any of us been the partner of Eve, we'd be just as fallen.

Sometimes a news item—perhaps a shooting on a campus, or a terrorist attack, or child abuse—stuns us, and we ask, "How could such a thing happen?" But our surprise only reveals our inadequate grasp of human nature. We human beings harbor a darkness, a seedy side; residing in even the purest soul is the potential to behave terribly. God's will is violated in horrific ways, and the truth is any one of us could be the perpetrator.

World Turned Upside Down

The problem with the world isn't merely the sum total of individual mistakes: whole systems, governments, corporations, and societies become riddled with ungodliness. History isn't exactly a chronicle of moral progress. Why do bad things happen? If we probed deeply, we would discover that a decent percentage of the "bad things" that happen can be chalked up to garden-variety human sinfulness (as we will see in chapter 6). Somebody does something God would prefer the person not do, and the result is suffering.

Or many somebodies together form a culture that is plunging headlong away from God, and God's will is obscured and hammered. And then the dead weight of large, corporate, societal sin worsens our individual proclivity to sin—and the vicious cycle swirls. We boldly work to rid the world of evil, but we shrug in resignation as each one of us is compelled to admit that "I cannot banish evil from my own heart."

We have Bibles, plenty of them, lying around on coffee tables. The truth is we are a bit leery of the Bible. A few years ago, a friend was about to purchase a sprawling lakefront mansion. Just to rib him a little, I asked, "Have you been praying about this decision?" He said, "Absolutely not! I thought, What would Jesus do? and I knew Jesus wouldn't buy this house." No hunch method? No reading of tea leaves? For a guy not so well versed in Bible, he surprised me by quoting Jesus himself: "Foxes have holes, and birds . . . have nests, but the Son of Man has nowhere to lay his head" (Matt. 8:20). Having dazzled me with the perfect verse, he admitted, "I just want to buy the house, so I'm not talking to Jesus about it." We do this all the time, deciding what I want to do and not inquiring too diligently into God's will.

The simple counsel of the Bible is doable, but hard, even countercultural. No one at work will applaud you for doing God's will. The Bible says to serve the poor. Did you do that yesterday? or last week? Jesus said, "Do not store up for yourselves treasures on earth" (Matt. 6:19). Are you in any small way trying to do God's will on that one? Mark Twain was laughably correct when he said that it wasn't the parts of the Bible he didn't understand, but those he did understand, that worried him.

God's will is so comprehensive! Supposing I do God's will in this decision, or in that situation. Fine—but God wants more. God is all-consuming. God's will, even if I am blind to the fact, extends its tentacles into every corner of my life, every room of my house, every synapse in my brain, the dollar bills in my wallet, the spare ten minutes I have just before dinner, the socks in my drawer, my vacation plans, the passing glance at a stranger. In a way, it is marvelous that God is everywhere, but then this omnipresence just makes getting God's will done even more impossible.

We may voice a holy intention: "I ought to pray more. I ought to read the Bible. I ought to volunteer. I ought to go on a diet."

Notice the wrinkle? "Ought" doesn't get you anywhere, does it? There is this paralysis hidden inside it: "I ought to pray," implying your real plan is to do no differently. The "ought" stirs up a little twinge of guilt, nothing more. So there is something ugly hidden inside this oughtness. How will we ever do God's will if we find ourselves paralyzed in the oughtness?

Not that we think for one moment of running up a flag of surrender! When he accepted the Nobel Peace Prize, Martin Luther King rather eloquently said, "I refuse to accept that the isness of man's current nature makes him incapable of reaching up for the eternal oughtness that forever confronts him."[1] Some people become passive, almost fatalistic: "What *is* is God's will." But this is not right. There is an isness that falls far short of the oughtness that God has for us.

I am not able to accomplish this oughtness. But at least I can recognize where it is, and where it isn't. The oughtness isn't the doctrinaire mores of society. The first Christians were accused of "turning the world upside down" (Acts 17:6)—which is what the world needs. God's will isn't just an improved version of what we find in our society. God's will is subversive; God's will usually is detectable as going against the grain of our culture. This is why we should expect preachers to "step on our toes." We need to develop a taste for the Church that loves enough to provide correction.

The Power and Mercy of God

But if we cannot do God's will, why bother? Because we believe in the power of God. We trust God. We let God do the work of a great sculptor, hacking at and chiseling us, liberating the beautiful person imprisoned in the stone of sin. We let God be a surgeon, for without submitting to the scalpel of God's surgical procedures, coping with the pain and working through convalescence to a renewed self, and even being drawn to the cross, we remain stuck in the paralysis of the status quo, and we will never know God's will, not to mention the abounding mercy of God.

We dissolve the sense of separation between our lives and God. In their popular book *Experiencing God: Knowing and Doing the Will of God,* Henry Blackaby and Claude King set up a conflict between "what I can do" and "what God does." For instance, they speak of "God-sized" assignments, and conclude, "If the assignment I sense God is giving me is something that I know I can handle, I know it probably is not from God."[2]

But why wouldn't God ask you to do something you can do? God probably wants me to clean up around the house, and I'm perfectly capable of doing so. We need not split up what is human from what is of God, because God became human, God made you and me as humans. Part of God's work is me, my brain, my muscle, my talents. I do not offer them to God the way a philanthropist offers excess wealth to the deserving poor. I simply look in the mirror, see what is in fact God's, and off we go.

And we laugh as we go, knowing we will fumble, tumble, and botch things. God is merciful, all is grace; God uses the bumbling. Our inability, when it plunges forward, becomes a great vessel for God, and we simultaneously discover the unstinting mercy of God. Humility should come naturally to us, and we have good cause to be merciful with ourselves, and with others: God is merciful to us.

Prayer, again, is the key—and I am constantly grateful for this duly famous prayer from Thomas Merton:

> My Lord God, I have no idea where I am going. I do not see the road ahead of me. I cannot know for certain where it will end. Nor do I really know myself, and the fact that I think I am following your will does not mean that I am actually doing so. But I believe that the desire to please you does in fact please you. And I hope I have that desire in all I am doing. I hope that I will never do anything apart from that desire. And I know that if I will do this you will lead me by the right road though I may know nothing about it. Therefore will I trust you always, though I may seem to be lost and in the shadow of death. I will not fear, for you are ever with me and you will never leave me to face my perils alone.[3]

We count on the mercy of God, and the hope that there is some tide that will carry us beyond what we are able to do or even the mistakes we have made. We hope that in history, despite all the debris of mistakes, wars, and chaos, God, with all good wisdom, power, and merciful love for the world that God has made, will carry us despite ourselves on some powerful divine tide to the dawn of the realization of God's kingdom.

I am moved when I think about St. Francis,[4] and how he discovered God's claim on his life. Daily, for many months, he went to a small, dilapidated church called San Damiano, and knelt before a crucifix, speaking to Jesus. Over and over he repeated the same prayer, waiting, listening, for days, weeks, months—jarring for us, who think we can Google God's will and it will pop up in a nanosecond. Francis prayed, kept praying, kept reading, kept listening. The words he used are as good a starting place as any for those of us who are serious about God's will:

> Most high,
> glorious God,
> enlighten the darkness of my heart
> and give me, Lord,
> correct faith,
> certain hope,
> perfect charity,
> wisdom and perception,
> that I may do
> what is truly your most holy will.

After countless repetitions of this prayer, over many months, during which time he suffered bouts of depression and various physical ailments, Francis finally heard Jesus speak back—and the rest is history.

We pray, perhaps this prayer from Francis, perhaps another. We rage against our culture and our own personal tendencies by persisting in prayer, sticking with it over time, waiting, trusting, blocking out time, insisting that our relationship with God is an inviolable priority.

What I adore about this particular prayer from Francis is the word *do*. Francis seeks light in his heart and mind, wisdom and insight—not just so he can mentally think about God's will. His only objective is "that I may *do* what is truly your most holy will." God's will is something I *do*, not a vague thought or speculative question I harbor. Impatient with the inertia of uncertainty or sinfulness, at some point you stop ruminating over God's will and you break the frozen ice, you do something, you launch out in hope— humble, a bit uncertain, but with a dogged determination to please God: no holding back! "Present your bodies as a living sacrifice. . . . Do not be conformed to this world, but be transformed by the renewal of your minds, so that you may discern what is the will of God" (Rom. 12:1–2).

God's will isn't generalized niceness, but something specific I believe God wants me to do. God wants me to do *this* with my life, and not *that*. God wants me to go *here*, not *there* this afternoon. I've practiced what I know God wants, I am sure God won't call me to do something that is alien to what God has made clear, and above all else I pray—and not a quickie prayer, but a focused appeal to God, one I make over and over until my receptiveness to God becomes second nature. I begin to have the mind of Christ (Phil. 2:5); I see as the Lord sees (1 Sam. 16:7).

Questions for Discussion

1. Where do you find "sin" getting in the way of God's will? In society? In your personal life?
2. Do you "consult Jesus" before making a decision? Why, or why not?
3. In what ways do you gain a sense of the specific things God want you to do?

Chapter Four

God's Will for Us

B ut I also become the hands, the feet of Christ, myself, but in good company with others; together we become the Body of Christ. Are we able to do this on our own? Of course not. But with God, nothing is impossible (Luke 1:37). For the one who is eager to know and do God's will, it becomes impossible to be alone. God's will, swept forward by the wonder of grace, is something we do with others.

It Is Not Good to Be Alone

The more serious I get about God's will, the more I discover that other people are involved. When I was a little boy, just six or seven years old, I suffered a bizarre psychological malady. I don't know how I came by this belief, but I was convinced I was the only person in the world. There appeared to be other people, but I thought it was like a movie being beamed into my head. Once I got to college and studied ancient philosophy, I learned that my thoughts back then had not been totally bizarre: in the fifth century BCE, several philosophers taught what I had believed as a child. They were "solipsists." For solipsists, you are the only thing you can be sure of; all you can know is yourself. At age seven, I'd been a budding solipsist.

But aren't all of us, in this culture, budding solipsists? You are taught from day one that you are on your own. You live in this

39

husk of yourself, and you perceive the world out there, but all that really matters is *me*. Other people exist for me and my pleasure. I value them based on whether or not they help me get where I am trying to go. Advertisers treat me as a valued solipsist: I must consume, it's all about me; I am the center of the universe. Solipsism invades our spiritual life, and our self-focus trumps in even when we ask good questions like *What is God's will for me?*

Once I decide solipsism isn't the truth about me, I begin to see what God meant at the very beginning of time by saying, "It is not good that the man should be alone" (Gen. 2:18). It is not good to think of God's will for the Lone Ranger, or Narcissus, or Silas Marner the lonely miser. What does God want me to do? What does God want *us* to do? And how do we help each other toward God's will and away from our solipsism?

If solipsism isn't God's will, then we begin to notice the ways we shrink God's will down to something that might be just too small. When I was in college, I wasn't a religious person, but some people invited me to church. I found there a group of students sitting on a floor, singing, listening to a spellbinding pastor. I had to admit it was great fun.

I noticed a young woman sitting near me, and she was very pretty. Just as I was hatching a plan to meet her when the program was over, they asked for prayer requests. Her hand shot up. I wondered, "What will this beautiful maiden request of God?" She said, "I want to give thanks to God, because I was running late the other day and couldn't find a parking place downtown. I asked God for help, and a car pulled out right in front of me." I pondered this briefly and thought, "I'll pass on talking to her." It just seemed so . . . small.

Surely God's will is something . . . big? or more weighty than the mere convenience of parking. Daniel Burnham, the great architect from a century ago, said, "Make no small plans, for they have no magic to stir the blood." God calls us to get our blood stirred, to dare something big for God. Even if you do something small for God, it's part of something big. You feed one hungry person, but the kingdom of God dawns; you teach Sunday school, gluing cotton onto construction paper, and it's Jesus, the Good

Shepherd; you don't misbehave in your marriage, and it's part of a broader adventure of saying to young people that marriage may in fact be a noble thing, a gift from God. We begin to dare big things for God, and we get the point of the little things that also are for God. Mother Teresa once said, "Every time I feed a hungry person, it's just a drop in the ocean, but the ocean would be one drop less without it."

But doesn't God care about little, seemingly trivial things? Jesus said God cares for sparrows, or a small lily in a field. So can't God find me a parking place? Recently I engaged in a parking-lot experiment as I contemplated the memory of the young woman I so briefly was drawn to years ago and this question about God's will, particularly God's relationship to parking. Driving about in various lots, I jotted down observations. Some people in large sports utility vehicles park just across the little white line, thereby occupying not one, but two places. Is it God's will for people to straddle the line and keep me (or someone more frail and elderly) from parking? Or is it God's will for us to park between the lines?

Sometimes a car pulled out in front of me. I noticed something important every time: behind the wheel of every car, there was a person. I wondered: What is God's will? Not for me as the parker, but for the other guy, the puller-outer? Did God make him pull out? What is going on in his life? What is God's will for him? A man backed out in front of me: was it God's will? I imagined a best-case scenario: he said a prayer in his office, and God told him to get moving and volunteer to tutor a disadvantaged child, so he took off. Clearly God's will was being done, and I got a space too. Another guy pulled out: was it God's will? I imagined a worst-case scenario: he had just been upstairs having a romantic tryst with somebody else's wife—so he shouldn't have been in that parking place to start with.

Friends and Family

These are silly ruminations. And yet, they remind me that I tend to think of God's will as being about me. But there are so many people out there. What is God's will for them? Does God rather cavalierly use them for my pursuit of the will of God? Or do they have their own agenda, their own issues?

We can forever ask, "What is God's will for me?" But we solipsists seeking God's will are drawn into a better question: "What is God's will for us?" You have friends. Do you ever gather and ask, "What is God's will for us?" Instead we ask about diversions: "Did you see the game? Been to any good restaurants? or movies?" But what is God's will for us?

What about families? We ask questions like "What would be fun to do today?" "What can we do to help our child build a good résumé for college? But what is God's will for us—as a family? A few Christmases ago, a small glimpse of God's will was revealed to us. For all prior holidays, we had witnessed what in retrospect I cannot fathom to be God's will: All the children gathered under the tree and opened presents; all the presents were gift cards, and they were wheeling and dealing the cards to get to shop where they wanted to buy ever more whimsical items. American Eagle? Borders? Christ is born—among gift cards?

One of the aunts got a better idea. Instead of swapping gift cards so the kids could browse the mall in a consumer frenzy, buying hip but unneeded items, the children could give each other gifts of mission. One by one, each child gave a different type of gift card, reporting a donation to some agency; each child had been required to have some personal involvement in the mission in question, so each child told a story about caring and how cool it had been. One gave her cousins a gift of mission for an AIDS orphanage in Kenya, and she told what it was like to go there; she passed around pictures and showed off her Kenyan necklace. Another child gave a gift of mission to a homeless shelter, where she had visited and served food. What is God's will for our family?

What is God's will for our church? Church is not a big crowd of solipsists, although we treat it that way, asking, "What's in it for me?" "Where's my piece of the church?" "Can I get my seat?" "Does the preacher suit me?" "Was my baptism a memorable experience?"

But what is God calling us to do—together, as a church, as the Body of Christ? We are baptized together into the Body; my salvation only makes sense as I find my place in Christ's Body. Together, as one Body, we are Christ down here on earth. You can't be Christ by yourself! You need those other body parts, the coordination of hand, foot, knee, elbow, hips, ribs, a holy collaboration. We love one another, we become the hands and feet of Christ in the world, we achieve more together than one of us could ever accomplish alone.

A question we did not delve into when we were exploring *What does God want me to do?* is vocational: What does God want me to do, not just today, or in this or that discrete decision, but with my life? What is God calling me to do with the bulk of my waking hours? When I started college, I had grand plans to be a scientist (or to veer into something in which I could make a lot of money), but God stunned me and everyone who knew me and I was morphed into a pastor. I have witnessed firsthand God calling many young people—and some not so young!—into dramatically new vocations.

We could spend a full chapter on how we probe this question of *What does God want me to do with my working life?* But it is never a merely personal, individual quest. Others are impacted in two ways. A lawyer once came to me and with riveting emotion explained that his God-given dream had been to teach high school and coach inner city kids. Having grown impatient with his very successful, lucrative, but hollow life as an attorney, he wanted to make a break. But what would his wife and teenaged children think? Or his clients? Or his elderly mother? What about the house, his network of commitments? My decision to be a pastor had a rolling effect on my parents, and now on my wife and children.

But it's more than that, isn't it? To ask, "What is God calling me to do?" implies that we care about making a difference in the world. In a career (or even, just a "job"), the goal is more money, a higher rung on the ladder, bigger office, more plaudits—for me. But a calling is very different. Calling implies a function within the broader community, and in fact a role in the betterment of the community. In the sentimental movie favorite *It's a Wonderful Life*, Mr. Potter thinks he can buy off George Bailey with a fat salary, the nicest house in town, some new dresses for Mrs. Bailey, and the occasional business trip to New York. But George storms out of Potter's office, back to his little building and loan, with little to show for his enormous efforts—except for a wonderful life and a different kind of Bedford Falls.

My grandfather was a rural mail carrier. But this wasn't a "job" to him; it was his "calling," and he delivered the mail as if on a mission from God. He took me with him many times, and along the route he would park the car and carry a bag of groceries in to someone who was bedridden, or hold hands and pray with someone from his church. I have no doubt that his beautiful embodiment of God's calling was readying me to respond to God's calling when the minister of the young woman who prayed for a parking place looked at me one day and asked what God was calling me to do with my life. I'd never heard the question before—but I had seen what the answer looked like.

In the company of others, when you do God's will, somebody else discovers God's will; somebody else is blessed. The reason I am writing this book about God's will is that somebody else did God's will, and then another person doing God's will asked me what God's will was for my life. He in turn did God's will because somebody else had done God's will to get him involved in God's will. It's lovely, isn't it?

Politics and Prayer

On my own, I tend to make jaded judgments, deceiving myself, pasting God's will on the outside of what is nothing but my own agenda. We need each other to discern God's will, for us and for me, and just how crucial this is becomes evident in perhaps the most hotly contested arena in which people dare to speak of God's will: politics.

Oddly, in this zone where we would expect modest uncertainty about the will of God and (given the nature of the separation of Church and state) a reticence to declare any political decision as emanating from the divine, we hear much cocksure talk about God: "God is on our side." "God endorses our policies." "God bless America." Charles Marsh has called this "promiscuous talk" that "humiliates God."[1] Politicians blabber on about God in less than flattering ways. Could our manipulative attachment of God to politics be what "taking God's name in vain" is about?

I happened to be on the dais once when a politician declared it had been God's will that he be elected, that God had assured him just before the election that his victory was guaranteed by God. Young and a bit impolite, I told him afterward that I had voted for his opponent—and I asked him "Was I sinning?" in doing so. "Oh, no," he backpedaled. God most clearly is not running elections down here on earth, or we wouldn't be in the messes we are in. God is not launching wars and advocating policies that shelter the pious who claim God is on their side. God cares profoundly about politics, and every decision; but God's ways are not our ways—God's ways are higher than our ways.

We have heard many political leaders say, "I have prayed about this, I believe God is telling me to pursue this war." The problem is that when any single person prays, refusing to let others who are praying weigh in on what they are hearing or even whether what was allegedly heard from God matches what we know about God from Scripture or not, we risk the absolutizing of one person's religious arrogance. Deeply bothered by President George W. Bush's claims that God led him into the Iraq war, Marsh pointed out that Bush portrayed himself "as one who has seen God face to face."

> He does not need church, tradition, or hierarchy; he is an intimate of God, God without mediation, God without the nuisance of tradition, God without doctrines and creeds. . . . If Jesus is only speaking to us as individuals, everything is then negotiable.[2]

Marsh, I would add, could have used the same words to describe countless leaders throughout history who have shamefully attached God to their political programs.

God speaks to individuals. But God does not *only* speak to us as individuals, and we as individuals hear God only in concert with the Church, centuries of tradition, our creeds. We need the test of conversation with others to discern God's will. Otherwise everything really is negotiable, and to speak of God's will is no better than for me to share my private biases.

We need not only each other, those at arm's reach, but those we have never met, people who live far from us. To think of God's will in the political realm, we need to consider something of a "global" test. God cares not merely about me and mine, or my country, but all the world, and the God of the Bible seems to have a soft spot in the divine heart for the poorest, the most disadvantaged, the people others steamroll or simply ignore.

To sharpen our perception, and become more adept at God's will, we submit ourselves to the routines of the Church, where we find friends, good company, a treasury of habits we Christians have found useful, having shaped millions of the faithful so they might know and do God's will together. We worship with others; Sunday by Sunday, we sing hymns together, we listen to Scripture and a sermon, we bow our heads, we shuffle forward for Communion with a holy host of others—and over time we are reshaped into somebody more like Christ, more attuned to God, not alone but together as the Body of Christ. In worship, power comes down on us and we are catapulted out of the sanctuary by an energy greater than any we possess to do the will of God, and to cope with the tragic. Without the Spirit's empowering presence we never accomplish or understand the will of God, and we are forever isolated as solo practitioners who never get the hang of God's will.

Mentors and the Poor

A crucial item we find in worship that we don't get at home alone is . . . other people. We do not first ask whether we like them or whether they share our socioeconomic background or tastes in music or cars. We need others, especially others who are different. We even need the friction that sparks among difficult people; friction smooths and polishes, so we might reflect God's glory. Without the people of God, their wisdom, counsel, questions, and love, we struggle poorly to know or do God's will. If you are wrestling with a decision, share your dilemma with Christians

who love you and are serious about God, and see what they have
to say. Every one of us needs wise mentors.

Or at least one. In graduate school I kept taking courses from
a professor, Fr. Roland Murphy, who became my adviser, and I
served as his teaching and research assistant. But beyond acade-
mics, he was a sage, a confidant, my spiritual father. I never made
an important decision without talking it over with him. His perspective, his ability to probe lovingly, his avoidance of all flattery,
his large vision for me and God and what might happen if the two
of us got together, all of this rendered him invaluable to my life.
Since his death, I have never found a replacement. I miss him, and
yet I still benefit from his example, his counsel, his lingering presence beyond the grave.

To discern God's will, we hang around people who do God's
will, or at least care enough to try hard. We mimic their moves,
the way little boys swing a bat like their heroes they have seen on
television. We seek out friends who will "speak the truth in love,"
who love frank conversation, who will share, speculate, suggest,
exhibit mercy, and at the end of the day go with us out into the
world to take a stab at doing God's will together.

God also places some unexpected helpers in our path: the poor,
and those who suffer. We misunderstand this gift: we think, "I'll
help the poor, that is God's will"—and it is. But the poor also
expose our own poverty, and thereby free us up to know we are
God's children, nothing more, nothing less. We think, "I pity
those who suffer"—and we should. But sufferers sober us up and
remind us of what matters and what doesn't. Spend time with the
poor, sit with friends and family who are hurting, and new win-
dows open into God's heart and will.

If we cultivate a simple attentiveness to the needs of the world,
the will of God presents itself in many guises. When the Nazis
conducted their genocide during World War II, an embarrass-
ingly small number of Christians harbored and rescued Jews
whom they did not even know. Asked why they risked everything,
most of them replied that they assumed God was active in their
world—so when a stranger knocked on the door desperate to hide,
these gentiles interpreted the opportunity as a sign from God, the

need of another person being the clearest conceivable indication of the will of God. What God wants may come knocking, or it may be right under our noses, and we help each other to notice, and then we and those to whom we reach out help each other to embody what truly pleases God.

For us to pursue God's will, we need to encourage each other, to value the quest for God's will in each other. Many of us need some healing, as we may harbor negative self-images that screen out the love of God; a crippling sense of inferiority makes it impossible to dare anything significant for God. Fear may overwhelm us, but our common passion for love and the will of God can overwhelm fear. Encouragers help others to do God's will, and thus do God's will themselves. And then big things happen. Our doing of God's will, in fact, had better be big, because evil vaunts itself and never rests, forcing us at every turn to face evil, to combat evil, to alleviate suffering, always prepared to ask that most daunting of questions: Why do bad things happen?

Questions for Discussion

1. Why is it important to realize others are involved in helping us know God's will?
2. Have you experienced instances when other people have helped you to know God's will? Have you helped others know God's will?
3. What dangers are there in associating one's particular political views with the will of God?

Part 2

Chapter Five

When Bad Things Happen

O ne of my favorite movie moments comes in *Steel Magnolias*. Shelby, a young mother, has died at age twenty-seven, leaving a young son behind. The mourners are drifting away after the burial, but Shelby's mother, played perfectly by Sally Field, lingers by the grave. Her friends notice, and gather to try to offer comfort. Truvy and Clairee say something about how pretty the flowers are, then stare at their shoes in awkward discomfort. Annelle, a young hairdresser who is quite devout, offers solace: "It should make you feel a lot better that Shelby is with her king. We should all be rejoicing."

Shelby's mother responds: "Well you go on ahead. I'm sorry if I don't feel like it. I guess I'm kind of selfish. I'd rather have her here." And then she begins to give voice to her ache, her horror, her total, exasperating agony, screaming from the marrow of her gut: "Why? Why? Why?" Screaming, sobbing, she literally hollers, "Oh God! I want to know Why? Why? Lord, I wish I could understand! It's not supposed to happen this way! I'm supposed to go first! I don't think I can take this!" Moviemaking has seldom portrayed such compelling emotion.

A question: Who was more faithful? Annelle, with her very true spiritual statements of faith? Or the mother, casting about in the dark, hurling unanswerable questions, incapable of absorbing what are supposed to be comforting words of faith?

When there is suffering, we ask, "Why?" It is usually a shriek, a sob: "Why?" Many people think "I know I shouldn't ask God, 'Why?' I should believe, but instead I just wonder, 'Why?'" Why shouldn't we ask "Why"? What did Jesus say on the cross? "My God, my God . . . Why?" We are not supposed to bear suffering under the slogan of Tennyson's Light Brigade: "Theirs not to reason why, / Theirs but to do and die." "Why?" isn't a rational question that would admit of a reasonable reply, is it?

We cannot fathom all that is tucked inside every "Why?" Sometimes it is the gasping reflex of having someone you never imagined living without ripped away from you. Sometimes it is the mind scouring a dark corner for any shred of meaning. In Amy Tan's novel *The Kitchen God's Wife*, a grown daughter recalls:

> My father had died of stomach cancer when I was fourteen. And for years, my mother would search in her mind for the causes, as if she could still undo the disaster by finding the reason why it had occurred in the first place. "He was such a good man," my mother would lament. "So why did he die?" Sometimes she cited God's will as the reason . . . She puts no faith in other people's logic—to her, logic is a sneaky excuse for tragedies, mistakes and accidents. According to my mother, *nothing* is an accident . . . Everything has a reason.[1]

But the disasters can never be undone. Pious words, no matter how theologically accurate they may be, only rub salt into an open wound. We cry out, "Why?" and find ourselves in a dark valley where logic cannot avail.

If we're honest, we say sugary things more for ourselves than for the one we think we are comforting. Annelle admitted as much to Shelby's mother; realizing she had enraged her, she apologized: "I don't mean to upset you. It's just that when something like this happens I pray very hard to make heads or tails of it. I feel much safer knowing she's up there on my side. It may sound real simple and stupid, and maybe I am. But that's how I get through things like this." But it's not about the onlookers or the friends, and it's not merely about feeling better. It's about the ache of the sufferer—and what is true. If we justify God to the face of someone who has lost what that person thought was God's most precious gift, we isolate the sufferer from God—just when he or she needs God the most. Jesus, in gruesome agony on the cross, cried in a loud voice, "Why?" No one answered him, not even God.

Weep with Those Who Weep

Why do bad things happen? Usually we add "to good people." But why? I hope I never become the sort of person who beams with pleasure when bad things happen to bad people. Why did God arrange the world where there would be disasters? Why did God make you and me with the shabby potential to hurt each other and ourselves? Why did God fashion a world in which mortality reigns? in which weariness bedevils us? Why Katrina? or 9/11? or the ugliness that transpired in my house just last night? We might ask, "Why?" not only when we witness atrocities in the news or agonize over the nausea from chemotherapy, but also when our lives seem so cozily arranged and people four miles away sleep under a bridge.

Why? Before we try to answer, we might be comforted to know that God isn't like a tired parent, wishing the children would stop asking, "Why?" God wired us in such a way that we cannot help asking. In fact, God wants us to ask, even to ask more, never turning off the searchlight probing the mystery of God's will. At the end of the book of Job, God does not applaud Job for figuring out why he was suffering; but God does seem to honor the fact that Job persistently continued to talk *to* God, not just *about* God,[2] railing, questioning, never shutting down the conversation, however one-sided it had to feel at times.

Jesus, interestingly enough, never gathered his disciples to say, "Okay, God inflicted evil for this reason. . . ." In the teeth of evil and suffering, Jesus *bore* suffering and evil: he wept, he grieved, he took evil onto his own body unjustly and was crucified. He formed a community that could shoulder one another's suffering, that could love as Jesus loved. And, he *resisted* suffering and evil: he chided profiteers who oppressed, he fed the hungry, he engaged in combat against the devil. He invites those of us he has left behind to resist evil in his name.

When we hear about a tragedy, or encounter someone's awful plight, we leap too quickly to declare, "Oh, it was God's will"—which has a way of shutting up the cry, the raging grief, the unanswerable question of the one who suffers. Instead of concocting some divine placebo of an answer that probably feels cruel to someone who has just lost a child or been slammed by life, we come, we shudder. "Weep with those who weep" (Rom. 12:15). We do not rush anyone to "feel better." We sit together in the dark and just listen to the muffled quiet. Otherwise, with our tidy answers that are too trivial to be true, we cut off the other person from exploring the darkness.

Why do bad things happen? raises perhaps an even more important question. What do we do *when* bad things happen? Early in his prolific teaching life, C. S. Lewis devised a logical rationale for why pain and evil happen, insisting that events that cause suffering are God's "hammer blows."

> God whispers to us in our pleasures, speaks in our conscience, but shouts in our pains: it is His megaphone to rouse a deaf world.[3]

To this young, cocksure Lewis, it is as if we are in a dazed stupor, so God uses horrors and suffering to wake us up, to bang us on the head and into submission to God.

But then Lewis married, and his wife, Joy, died after a brief but terrible bout with cancer. Having lived through such a loss, he no longer spoke of pain and suffering as God's hammer blows. He understood the way the painful loss of love is too overwhelming to be reduced to some logical formula. Sharing his struggle, Lewis wrote *A Grief Observed*, and on its first page we overhear a clue to what we should do when bad things happen.

> No one ever told me that grief felt so like fear. I am not afraid, but the sensation is like being afraid. The same fluttering in the stomach, the same restlessness, the yawning. I keep on

swallowing. At other times it feels like being mildly drunk, or concussed. There is a sort of invisible blanket between the world and me. I find it hard to take in what anyone says. Or perhaps, hard to want to take it in. It is so uninteresting.[4]

Then he points the way for us in our ministry of healing: "Yet I want the others to be about me. I dread the moments when the house is empty. If only they would talk to one another and not to me."

As Christians, we are peppered with hard questions about why bad things happen from people who despise God, or who used to believe in God, or who are struggling to believe in God. The litmus test is not whether we can craft clever theological explanations, but whether we love, whether we show up. Why do bad things happen? We can talk about that later, but while the news is fresh we bake cakes and deliver casseroles, we send notes that say "I love you," we just sit in the den, we hug, we pray, we think all day long about the one we love who has lost the one she loved.

We continue to remember, even months later, after the other mourners have drifted away. Silent suffering, constant presence, and not merely for a day or two after the awful news breaks. Sorrow is its most piercing on some unanticipated day five weeks after the other mourners have returned to their routines, or three years later—but didn't the grief book say that getting over a loss is a process that can take up to two years? What is God's will? as in, What does God want us to do? We show up: an economy of words, a maximum of presence. We love.

Carried by the Faith of Others

When bad things happen to *us*, we hope others show up. If they do, we trust them, we let them love us, we are patient when they say dumb but well-intended things. God fumed that Job's friends bombarded him with bad theology—but then asked Job to pray for them (Job 42:7–8)! We may be at a loss over what to think or believe about God. I may look into my gut and find no faith at all, the pain is so acute. And in these moments, others can and will believe for me.

Jesus healed a paralytic who had been hauled by four other people onto a roof, then lowered quite passively before Jesus. Intriguingly, Mark 2:5 reports: "When Jesus saw their faith, he . . ." *Their* faith? The faith of others can carry us when we have no faith. The Church is most itself when believers carry those who don't have an ounce of faith energy left, whose tears block their view of God, who for the moment are the wounded leg in the Body of Christ, for which the Body then compensates with extra effort from the other members of the Body to keep moving toward God.

To me, the most profound of all the psalms is the 73rd, which raises pointed questions about suffering. Why do the wicked prosper? Why do those whose hearts are pure bear a seemingly disproportionate amount of agony? The psalmist, recalling how exasperating such feelings have been, articulates what many of us may have felt:

> But as for me, my feet had almost stumbled,
>   when I saw the prosperity of the wicked.
> For they have no pangs;
>   their bodies are sound and sleek.
> Always at ease, they increase in riches.
> (Ps. 73:2–12 RSV)

His dejected conclusion?

> All in vain have I kept my heart clean. . . .
> For all day long I have been stricken.
> (Ps. 17:13–15 RSV)

But notice the stunning turn in verse 17: "until I went into the sanctuary of God." We may harbor some fantasy that the "until" will soar upward to something like "until I was healed, until I won the jackpot, until everything returned to normal." But the psalm is more sober: "until I went into the sanctuary of God." When we suffer, we need a break, an interruption, some intervention, a safe harbor. So we go to the sanctuary, not because there is magic in the room. In the sanctuary, we try to remember what God has already willed. The sanctuary reminds us that God created everything, but it's not entirely safe out there—which is why the church earned the name "sanctuary."

The sanctuary has a Bible, so we listen to stories of saints and martyrs who have suffered and now rest in peace with God. The sanctuary is the manger in which we discover the Christ child, Emmanuel, God with us. The sanctuary has its prayers, giving form to our grief, enabling us to express our cry before God, yet containing it, managing it in the rhythm of worship.

The sanctuary also has people, the community, our church "family," whose faith carries us, whose prayers envelop us, whose constant labor is to alleviate suffering, who have suffered themselves, whom we have comforted and will comfort some other day, and more tenderly because of the pain we bear today.

And then we see the cross, we understand how God was not immune to the kind of suffering we know. We look to Jesus, who is the answer to both our questions: *What do you want me to do?* and *Why do bad things happen?* Maybe we begin to recall that God was not a manipulator in making the world, that evil has not been banished just yet, that God is not the heavenly Granddaddy making everything cozy for us. We recall that God came down in Jesus, who wept, and cried out, and breathed his last; Mary wept at the sight of her son dying an untimely, unjust death, and the whole scene is God's shoulder extended to us so we can fall on it and have a long cry.

Whom to Blame?

When bad things happen, we may blame ourselves for whatever has happened. "I should have taken him to the doctor sooner. I should have seen this coming. God must be punishing me for what I did." In moments of suffering, we have to battle zealously to remember the grace and mercy of God, that God isn't a tyrant lashing out, that God isn't negligent, that we live in a fallen world where, as George Eliot put it, "Perhaps nothing 'ud be a lesson to us if it didn't come too late."[5]

We need to hear God's gentle whisper: "I don't blame you. I am with you." Lots of times, the crushing burden of blame comes from those who should be loving the sufferer, but instead cannot resist that wicked urge to offer some banal theological rationalization for evil. Be careful: In our talk about suffering and God, we cannot let ourselves blame the sufferer.

We never really mean to. But there is this bogus spirituality that declares, "If you just have enough faith, if you just pray enough, you will be healed, or all will be well." I cannot think of a bigger lie within all of Christendom—and it's a lie that is just plain cruel. "If my cancer advances, . . . If I lose my job, . . . If my marriage unravels, I must not have had enough faith, I must not have prayed enough." It can't be God's fault, can it? God is in control—right? And since we have to protect God from blame when things go sour, whom is left to blame? Me.

Rightly, Christians think prayer is a fantastic, helpful activity. For us, prayer is like breathing; we would not dream of going very long without speaking and listening to God. But why do we believe that if we turn up the volume of prayer, the intensity of prayer, if we pray with some formula (like "I claim the victory") or if we pray in massive numbers (and with e-mail, prayer chains can spawn tens of thousands of links very quickly), that God will really have no choice but to yield? Have we read the Bible? Was Jesus a "prayer warrior" in Gethsemane, demanding God to "let this cup pass, and I claim this prayer shall be answered"?

Clearly God does not seem to favor the holy while trouncing the impious. What did Jesus tell the disciples? Some Jews were slaughtered by Pilate, leading Jesus to ask his disciples if they thought those who died were "worse sinners than all other Galileans" (Luke 13:2). In another news flash, eighteen were killed when a tower collapsed in Siloam. "Do you think they were worse offenders?" Jesus' answer is No. Repeatedly, Jesus, and the psalmists, and Paul differentiate between goodness or faith or prayer and what actually unfolds. The Bible knows unjust suffering, and the Bible knows how scoundrels succeed. Read Psalm 73: the holy who pray are in agony, while the slick unrighteous are healthy and at ease.

We guard our thoughts and words, and firmly refuse to blame the sufferer. But what about God? If we cry to God, if God is God, if God can answer, if God is involved, then is it God's fault? Doesn't God make everything happen? It must be God's fault— or God must not be so powerful if evil can run amok, if the suffering among God's children rages unchecked. Or God must not be so loving, if God sees that our hearts will be shattered but then stands by idly. Of course, if we suspect God isn't powerful, and if we further suspect God isn't loving, then we are teetering on the edge of the cliff that looms over the canyon of God's failure, not simply failure to do this or that, but failure even to exist at all. Is there a God at all? And if there is a God, then when bad things happen we have to ask, we are invited to ask, we are by faith itself compelled to ask: Why?

Questions for Discussion

1. Why is it important to "weep with those who weep" in the face of human suffering?
2. In what ways have you experienced being "carried by the faith of others"?
3. How can we resist "blaming the sufferer" when bad things happen?

Chapter Six

Why Bad Things Happen

I f you are reading this book and your spouse died of a heart attack last week, or if your daughter is in the throes of cancer, put this book down and come back to it in a year or two, and then read the rest of this chapter. Our tears help us to see the world and life as God sees things, but what we are about to walk through is a calm, compassionate, yet matter-of-fact assessment of why bad things happen. We can reason through this best when we're not in the thick of disaster. Try to engage in a little rational analysis of the causes of war when a grenade has just exploded next to you in a bunker. No, wait until you are back home and the bullets aren't flying. Wait until the grief has subsided a bit.

If you are ready, though, let us ask: "Why do bad things happen?" The truth is, we know why. If we apply our minds, we can sort through the reasons why each and every bad thing happens, and why the whole accumulation of bad things happen. Suffering may be unjustifiable or unspeakable, knee-buckling or emotionally jarring, but that does not mean suffering is unexplainable. There is always an explanation—which doesn't alleviate the pain, or let God off the hook. But we know why bad things happen.

Everything Happens for a Reason

Before we answer *Why do bad things happen?* let's back up and ask, "Why does anything at all happen?" To understand God's relationship to bad things, we need to avoid isolating this or that bad (or good!) event from everything else that goes on. The fact that you are reading, the grass is growing in the yard outside the window, the clouds are gathering, the dog is barking, an interruption kept you from getting into this chapter, the ache in your left knee throbs, the worry you thought was safely tucked into the back corner of your heart whispers, the news bulletin is overheard from the television in the next room, your memories alternately make you blush with joy or sigh with sorrow: everything, somehow, rests in God's hands. God is not removed from anything, anywhere. Jesus said of even the sparrows, "Not one of them will fall to the ground apart from your Father" (Matt. 10:29); and to impoverished peasants he said, "Even the hairs of your head are all counted" (Luke 12:7).

Why do bad things happen? People say, "Everything happens for a reason." Usually that word "reason" feels mystifying, perhaps pregnant with divine intent, as if God has some reason for causing a bad thing to happen but hasn't divulged it, or we haven't figured out that reason just yet. But as we have said throughout this book, God is not secretive. God takes no delight in our confusion. Everything does happen for a reason, and we can know the reasons.

We never for a moment corner God and pretend we have God figured out. But we can know the reasons why events happen. God's mind blows my mind. But the reasons for cancer or a car wreck my mind can handle, although my heart may not be able to.

Why do bad things happen? Let's first brush aside a common explanation that is just plain wrong, a well-intended but blasphemous reason that can be banished by our God-given reason. A car accident took my spouse; cancer besieged my mother; my son was killed in a random shooting. People swiftly say, "It was God's will." But was it really?

While suffering is never funny, we might turn to something that was in the comics a few years back. Gary Larsen, whose wit turned life on its ear with his daily *Far Side* strip, once imagined "God at his computer." On the monitor screen there is a guy walking down the sidewalk. Over his head, a few stories up, a piano is hanging by ropes, dangling precariously out of a window, presumably being hauled down by the piano movers. God's finger lingers over one of the computer keys which bears the word "Smite." Does God smite the guy? Or let him off?

But God does not smite guys with pianos. God does not sow cancer cells in people's bodies. God does not hurl automobiles into one another. God does not set a tornado to swirling and then point it at a particular neighborhood. God does not guide the scope and press the trigger finger so your sister gets shot. God does not invent AIDS to bludgeon homosexuals and drug users—any more than God inflicts people who indulge in high cholesterol diets with heart disease, or those who go outdoors on icy days with the sniffles.

In the Middle Ages, the great plague, which wiped out more than one quarter of the population of Europe, was thought to be God's wrath unleashed, as people did not understand how bacteria, fleas, and rats could conspire to kill so many. In the eleventh century, Christian prelates launched a great crusade against Muslims in Palestine, with the rallying cry, *Deus vult!* God wills it! Armed Christians bearing not very holy crosses arrived outside Jerusalem, and did as Israel did when arriving at Jericho centuries earlier: they blew trumpets and marched around the city, but the walls didn't go a-tumblin' down. So they enacted what they were sure was God's will, breaching the walls, then slaughtering the inhabitants. *Deus vult?*

Is "God willed it" the answer to "Why do bad things happen?" Hardly: God hates, God despises, God grieves every act of evil, all human suffering. God will lead the celebration when cancer is finally cured. God champions car safety. God wants us to get away from storms. God does good, and God only does good. "Every good . . . and every perfect gift is from above, coming down from the Father of lights, with whom there is no variation or shadow due to change" (James 1:17 RSV).

We get confused about this, partly because we want to cling to God and to avoid the notion that evil is on the loose. God only does good? We puzzle over this, in part because we are not very adept at determining what is good and what isn't good. A shifty businessman wins a million dollars. Did God do this "good" thing? But is winning a million dollars good? Are lots of the happenstances we rank as good really so good? Perhaps they poison the soul, and perhaps what is genuinely good appears to be a failure or a problem.

Part of understanding God's will is learning what is of God and what isn't, being able to distinguish between what is a blessing and what is only something I prefer, getting the knack of separating what the world thinks is a waste of time and yet is an essential ingredient in the life of faith from what the world prizes highly but really only ruins your soul. Jesus did say strange things like "Blessed are the poor. . . . Blessed are those who mourn. . . . Blessed are the meek. . . . Blessed are those who are persecuted" (Matt. 5:1–10).

So if God does not "smite," if God does not hurl down thunderbolts like the mythological deities of ancient Greece and Rome, if God is not a vengeful twit acting out old grudges, then why do bad things happen? Let us think back to when God was young, or to the time when God had some more age on him and decided to make the world.

Why Do We Sin So Much?

God never accepted a job description that dictates that God should always shelter me and make me healthy. God does not manipulate life on this planet, and so we need not be surprised when evil strikes. C. S. Lewis once estimated that four-fifths of humanity's suffering is inflicted by our fellow human beings. While this will strike many people as an absurd thought, it is sadly the case that human nature, left free by God to love God and to be magnificent, but also to ignore God and be downright ugly, is the cause of unspeakable suffering and evil in this world. Not all the suffering in the world by any means! But wars, terrorist attacks, extramarital affairs, crime, feelings of being unloved: we human beings hurt each other in wildly divergent, painful ways. We need not blame

God. Instead of asking, "Why do bad things happen to good people?" we ask, "Why do God's children sin the way they do?"

Of course, many thinkers who engage in the enterprise of "theodicy," defending God in the face of suffering, rely on our freedom as the explanation for bad things happening. Freedom is a portion of the answer, but certainly can't begin to explain why a tornado touches down and kills a child. And when we speak of freedom, we must be careful not to indulge in a little unwitting swagger. We prize freedom so highly, but we aren't as free as we like to think. Our freedom has been squandered, misused, wasted; we have made so many bad choices that now our will is in bondage to sin. We are driven by habits we cannot break. Our broader societal customs become the ruin of ourselves and others. Freedom leads to sin, but our shackled will, our fallen nature, leads to more disastrous sin, with the complication that, like an alcoholic, we can't just say no any longer.

After 9/11 people wondered what God was up to. Was God punishing America? Or did God just sleep in that morning? God does not sleep in, but God also does not hold up shields of protection around our buildings, or around our lives. If 9/11 was God's will, if God planned it, perpetrated it, and was pleased by it, then we should have nothing to do with God, and frankly, instead of hunting down terrorists to arrest and try them, we should give them ticker-tape parades and elevate them to sainthood because they did God's will. There are sins of commission, words and deeds of which we are all guilty, that explain much suffering and evil.

But there are also sins of omission. Think of what we could do, if only we were more serious about God's will. People ask me, "Why is there so much suffering in the world?" Part of the answer is that we, God's people, sit on our hands. We wash our hands and go to a nice dinner. When we sit down, we have a prayer. We thank God for our blessings and the lovely food that we are about to eat. If we are especially shrewd at our prayers we say, "Lord make us mindful of those who are less fortunate than we are." I always imagine God in heaven shouting back to us: "I don't want you to be *mindful* of those who are less fortunate; I want you to *do* something!" But we are too busy digging into the food to hear.

This is uncomfortable to talk about, isn't it? The tragic fact is that all of us who debate the question *Why do bad things happen?* have passed up a multitude of opportunities to get engaged in the world; had we seized our chances to do God's will, the net effect would be fewer bad things happening to cause us to ask about God's will. Children starve, not because God withholds food from portions of the globe, but because we haven't gathered the will to share our food. Somebody gets shot, perhaps by a teenager some Christian church might have mentored and cared for—and the love just might have staved off a crime.

We do not know how to be a peacemaking people, so perhaps the horrors of war germinate in our unholy conviction that the only solution to conflict is force. The people of God sin, sometimes actively, at other times by simply doing little to nothing. Only God knows how high the percentage of bad things that happen can be chalked up to sin, but the relationship between the two will of God questions—*What does God want me (or us) to do?* and *Why do bad things happen?*—is hauntingly close.

We can know why countless bad things happen, and we can know we can do better, despite our compromised nature. We strive to do God's will, more determined than ever once we contemplate when and why bad things happen. If food winds up on the table and I give thanks to God, what do I make of the unpleasant fact that food somehow hasn't gotten onto the table of another child someplace else, like the Sudan or a poor neighborhood in the city where I live?

I am getting the hang of this now: God certainly has good intentions for everything that goes on. Much of the time, God's good intent is realized. The rain falls, the wheat matures, and a hungry child enjoys bread. But so often, God's good intent is not realized. God's good will is frustrated. God's good will is even perverted, and suffering is rampant. God has given us plenty. Maybe it's God's will for us to be the ones who divide it up more capably, more generously, less greedily—and then we've answered, for at least a few, the problem of why some bad things happen, and we've discovered what God wants us to do.

Accidents Happen

Even the good things people do wreak havoc. How many human inventions unwittingly cause harm? One day we will know why cancer happens, and there is a reasonable chance that some wonderful human invention (could it be fluorescent lights or preservatives or something unseen like a wireless device?) is the culprit. How many natural disasters are either caused by or made worse because of what we have done to the "natural" world God made that isn't as "natural" as it once was?

When we invented the automobile, we signed an unwitting contract with death, because it's just dangerous to hurl tons of metal down the highway at high speeds, in proximity to other vehicles; driver error, mechanical failure . . . and you have suffering. The Amish never die in car accidents, because they never signed onto the risk contract that accompanies cars. God does not cause car accidents.

"Accident" is precisely the word. Accidents happen. Faith understandably feels an urge to say, "There are no accidents." Rick Warren, in his runaway bestseller *The Purpose Driven Life*, wrote

> You are not an accident. God prescribed every single detail of your body. He chose your race, the color of your skin, your hair, he determined your natural talents, he decided when you would be born and how long you would live. Traumas happen to shape your heart.[1]

Superficially, these thoughts seem reassuring if you are healthy, you have a job and you live in a family that loves you. But did God prescribe every single detail of the body of the child with cystic fibrosis, battling for every breath? Did God decide how long you would live and then inspire a crazed person to fire a rifle into a crowd because someone else's time was up? Did God ignite a civil war in the Sudan so the children of Darfur would suffer divinely ordained misery?

There is something accidental about all of us, and about the way life unfolds. The assembly line turns out cars, and we know some small percentage are going to have breakdowns. It's pure chance who gets one of them. God isn't in the factory preselecting you to get the lemon.

In the hour of death, Christians are prone to declare, "It was his time to die," as if when you were born God turned over an hourglass with a predetermined amount of sand that has finally seeped into the bottom. But if we think thoroughly about this, we see again we are casting God as a killer, using guns or cars or disease like an alarm clock buzzing us: "Time's up."

A few years ago, I suffered the loss of a very close friend, a young woman who planned to go to seminary. My phone rang, and the news buckled my knees: Molly had been killed instantly in a car crash. Did God kill her? Absolutely not. On the other side of the interstate, a car (for what reason? Simply drifting a little due to weariness? Changing a CD?) bumped another car, and the force at high speed sent that car out of control and across the median. Dozens, even hundreds of cars were passing that place that day. The car hit Molly. Did God select Molly to be struck? Did God cause the first driver to change the CD? It was an accident.

I always want to say (and I would be correct) that when some chance occurrence happens, you should not take it personally. But what could feel more personal? The cards are dealt, one person gets a readily curable heart condition, another gets the rare, incurable leukemia; one person wins the lottery, the other walks into the wrong store at the wrong time and gets mugged. It's accidental—you know it could happen to anybody at any time. Yet it's intensely personal.

Events can be personal without being dictated by God. There is such a thing as luck; history's greatest writers, from Sophocles to Shakespeare, have probed the side of our human predicament we call "tragedy." Bad luck (or even good luck) might feel like fate, or God's plan. But God isn't looking down, doling out good-luck and bad-luck cards. God is a communion of love, a fellowship of Father, Son, Holy Spirit, not a lone hacker conniving to corrupt the files of our lives.

The Nature of Our World

We live in a fallen world. And however well we grasp that a sizable percentage of suffering can be chalked up to human sinfulness, or human ineptitude, or just rotten luck, we still have some hard questions for God. The very fact of our mortality, of our physical vulnerability, not to mention the nemeses of disease and natural catastrophes: Why do we—as people who love, who get attached to other people and places, who hurt so much when someone we love dies—why do we have to face so much suffering?

To ponder these hard questions, we need to rewind in our minds—again!—to that point when God was young, when God made the world. If we read books about science, or go to the observatory, or poke around the Internet, we can learn more about what God has made. In a way, this is how God answered Job, who had suffered horrifically and hurled questions toward heaven. God took him on a tour of all that God had made, the universe at its most massive—and yet microscopic life at its finest exhibits a complexity of mind-boggling beauty and wonder that you could spend your lifetime exploring and never marvel at more than one-millionth of it all.

But this world that God made has a dangerous edge to it. The world is stupendous, but part of what is awesome is the presence of storms, wind, the risk, the peril. You're safe reading right now—but the world obviously isn't totally safe, never was, never will be. God's will was not for us to dwell in a bubble of security, and the beauty and meaning in it all would be lost in such a bubble.

I love to watch the waves rhythmically washing toward me on the beach from the expanse of ocean stretching to a distant horizon. But any beachcomber can tell you that the water is dangerous. So why then are we stunned by floods or hurricanes that wreck homes on the shore? Somehow we have hatched a false view of God as the Guarantee of my safety and well-being—but God made our world full of contingencies. It's risky down here.

After Katrina, people said God was punishing New Orleans for its citizens' raunchy lifestyle. But people behave badly in Kansas and Nebraska, Switzerland and Sierra Leone. New Orleans was dangerous because water is powerful, and storms happen. For decades, residents (like my own wife when she studied at Tulane) looked at the levees and fretted that someday one would break and the city would be flooded. God did not hurl a storm at anybody in particular, or you and I would be flooded out before we finish reading this book.

God built mortality into the fiber of things. The Bible declares that "the wages of sin is death" (Rom. 6:23), but death runs even more deeply. Death is everywhere. We are troubled by any human death, as we should be. But if you consider nature, death is normal, death is omnipresent, death is the healthy cycle of the universe. David Bentley Hart spoke eloquently of this:

> The natural world overwhelms us with its splendor, its beauty, its immensities and fragilities, its incalculable diversity, its endless combinations of the colossal and the delicate, sweetness and glory . . . But at the same time, all the splendid loveliness of the world is everywhere attended by death.[2]

Consider the life span of the amoeba, or that housefly you failed to swat. Deer, such elegant creatures, go off into the woods and die out of sight, as do many creatures who die daily. What is the food chain but a continuous domino-like tumbling of creatures into the jaws of death? The food we eat suffered death. Vegetarians don't want animals killed so we can eat; but vegetables and fruit die so we can eat. Death is normal, death is everywhere.

Diseases Not Yet Curable

The human body is a marvel, but all our bodies have imperfections, quirks, flaws. If I have little hair, people tell bald jokes. But if I have a weak heart, no one laughs—but should we blame God? God does not sow cancer cells in the body of your husband or lace your daughter's blood with leukemia. Our bodies are rickety, breaking down all the time. Clearly, we are not designed so that every person will live in sleek health, with muscular agility, until age one hundred.

Sometimes when we watch the news or get a phone call, we learn of a death, or many deaths, and we are shocked. In a way we should be; but then if we have a genuine understanding of human nature, we remember that we are all of us mortal, and in a way the surprise might be that we have made it safe thus far.

The march of science has postponed death, lengthening life— although at times we ponder the wisdom in prolonging life, even though we understand the desire to prolong the life of the one you love. But might it be more merciful to let death take its natural course more often than we do and to allow the dying to say good-bye and bless the living?

How interesting it is that only in modern times, when medicine has advanced astronomically, we have come to think of death as a reason to reject God. In ancient times, nobody doubted God if a young person died. Life expectancy was around thirty years; half your children routinely died at birth or soon after, as did a painfully high percentage of the mothers.

A century ago, infections were dumbfounding, and people died from simple cuts. Smart people devised antibiotics, and now we don't think twice about most infections. One day we will under-stand why cancer happens, and some medicine will fix it. Then no one will question God about cancer, any more than we do about infections today. But there will still be new diseases, new causes of our old nemesis, death.

It may then be helpful to remember that the mood of our cry *Why?* is a modern concern, and experienced most often by people with comfortable, sheltered lives. Had medicine not been so suc-cessful, we would have fewer questions about God. Perhaps we can also then see that God is more than a physician's helper, some-thing above and beyond a filler of the gap in our current knowl-edge of causes and cures.

As a pastor, I presided over the funerals of not one, not two, but three children in a single family. A rare, virulent leukemia was treated three different ways, failing each time. A tumult of grief ensued, and many who knew the family wondered how there could be a God if so much loss were sustained by a single pair of parents. I loved the children, and still grieve their deaths; I too felt the *Why?*

At the funeral, trying to help friends and family think through such staggering loss, I recalled visiting an old cemetery where I photographed the tombstones of three children in a family. Each stone had these profound little hymn lines etched: "Little ones to Him belong; They are weak, but He is strong."

They had died about one hundred years ago, all three from diphtheria. Back then, no one knew what to do about diphtheria, and many children died from it. Science caught up to the disease, and now deaths from diphtheria (at least in the Western world) are rare. One day we will know how to cure (or even prevent) the leukemia that felled my friends. Today we do not know the cure— but if we ask, "Why did they die?" we know the answer to the question. God did not kill them, or fail to save them. Bodies break down, illness happens; many diseases we can cure, some we will be able to cure but cannot just now. Yet even when we can cure that leukemia, it will be something else, some new disease, something.

Beauty in Light and Shadow

Even in suffering and death, there is a beauty. Were this the month of October, we would see death all around us in the form of leaves perishing, coming to the end of their days on the trees, fluttering down to the ground. We delight in the beauty of the color of death, a blanket of yellow, orange, and brown, hues of red amid lingering green in God's good world. Spend some time with people who have been by the bedside in the hour of death of someone they have loved. Through the grief, through the tears, they will tell you that it was beautiful, that it was an awesome privilege to be there.

When I was a boy, I spent every summer with my grandparents in the small town of Oakboro in rural Stanly County, North Carolina, not far from Big Lick and Frog Pond. If heaven is anything like churning ice cream under the old oak tree in my grandparents' yard with cousins and neighbors, I will not be disappointed.

One dark night, a few hours away from my grandparents, the telephone in our home rang. My parents roused me and my sister out of bed. We had to go to Oakboro—now, not in the morning, but now. We drove through the darkness, and into the sunrise. Not long after dawn, we pulled up in front of the house. My sister and I peered through the back window and saw our dad walk up to his brothers, all strong men, military veterans—and they fell on each other's shoulders and cried out loud.

Did we grieve my grandfather's death? Heavily. We still do, decades later. But there was beauty: I learned that day that life is precious, that love runs deep. How could such a thing happen to a boy like me? And yet, what a gift: to have had him at all, to have loved, to have been there to see the pain of his sons and the way we gathered on the third day in the Oakboro Baptist Church, on cue, offering our tears to God, entrusting him to God, and then going back home, to live, to love.

Isn't love always like that? C. S. Lewis, shortly after realizing his wife, Joy, was dying, wrote to the mystery writer Dorothy Sayers: "We soon learn to love what we know we must lose."[3] He had been right, years earlier, when he had said "The only place outside heaven where you can be perfectly safe from all the dangers and perturbations of love is hell."[4] The loss feels like hell, but love learns to lose, and hidden in the tissue of our grief is a peculiar beauty.

If we doubt such a seemingly bizarre thought, just remember: death is excruciatingly grievous, but lurking in the shadows is a surprising beauty, because the death of Jesus, our brother and our Lord, is beautiful. Those who passed by saw only ugliness and shame, and the horror and sorrow were immense; but the eyes of faith are stunned by the beauty of the cross. Jesus, his perfect body, all loving, all holy, nailed to an olive shaft which must have trembled with all of nature under the weight of his sacrifice, his blood poured out, sorrow and love flow mingled down, the water from his side, the river that makes glad the city of God, the healing of the nations, a window thrown open into the very heart of God, the turning point of history, the light that banishes every darkness. Yes, death is the "last enemy to be destroyed" (1 Cor. 15:26), and the certain anticipation of its defeat, won by Christ already, is beauty.

Let me close this section with a long, yet moving, eloquent passage from Karl Barth's *Church Dogmatics*:

Light exists as well as shadow. Creation has not only a positive but also a negative side. It belongs to the essence of crea-
turely nature, and is indeed a mark of its perfection, that it has
in fact this negative side. In creation there is not only a Yes but
also a No; not only a height but also an abyss; not only clarity
but also obscurity; not only growth but also decay; not only
opulence but also indigence; not only beauty but also ashes;
not only beginning but also end. In the existence of man there
are hours, days and years both bright and dark, success and
failure, laughter and tears, youth and age, gain and loss, birth
and sooner or later its inevitable corollary, death. In all this,
creation praises its Creator and Lord even on its shadowy side.
For all we can tell, may not His creatures praise Him more
mightily in humility than in exaltation, in need than in plenty,
in fear than in joy? May not we ourselves praise Him more
purely on bad days than on good, more surely in sorrow than
in rejoicing, more truly in adversity than in progress? If there
may be praise of God from the abyss, night and misfortune . . .
how surprised we shall be, and how ashamed of so much
unnecessary disquiet and discontent, once we are brought to
realize that all creation both as light and shadow, including
our own share in it, was laid on Jesus Christ, and that even
though we did not see it, while we were shaking our heads that
things were not very different, it sang the praise of God just
as it was, and was therefore right and perfect.[5]

The will of God is Jesus Christ, the light of the world, who suffered the darkest agonies, the very intersection of the brightness
of God and the shadow of sin and death.

Why do bad things happen? We cry, "Why?"—and in calmer,
more rational moments, we know why, although the pain is hardly
alleviated by whatever the answer is. Notice what we have not
even tried to do in this chapter: through history, theologians have
practiced "theodicy," the intellectual attempt to justify the goodness of God in the face of suffering and evil. We aren't explaining
away suffering as somehow good, and we aren't letting God off
any imaginary hook.

To use our minds to explain why car crashes or cancers happen isn't a defense of God, because we still have to ask the most important question: *Where* is God? The answer to *Why do bad things happen?* is only mildly helpful unless we can answer the only inquiry that matters to the heart: *Where was God? Where is God? Where will God be? Will God's will ever be done?*

Questions for Discussion

1. Why is it important to recognize that God "grieves every act of evil, all human suffering"?
2. In what ways are our "sins of omission" tied in with suffering in the world?
3. Is being able to answer "why bad things happen" fully satisfying to us? Why, or why not?

Chapter Seven

Where Is God?

A fter his son died when his car plummeted into Boston Harbor, William Sloane Coffin preached a sermon in which he declared,

> When a person dies, there are many things that can be said, and at least one thing that should never be said. The night after Alex died, a woman came by carrying quiches. She shook her head, saying sadly, "I just don't understand the will of God." Instantly I swarmed all over her. "I'll say you don't, lady! Do you think it was the will of God that Alex never fixed that lousy windshield wiper, that he was probably driving too fast in a storm? Do you think it is God's will that there are no streetlights along that stretch of road?" Nothing so infuriates me as the incapacity of intelligent people to get it through their heads that God doesn't go around with his finger on triggers, his fist around knives, his hands on steering wheels. God is dead set against all unnatural deaths. The one thing that should never be said when someone dies is, "It is the will of God." My own consolation lies in knowing that it was *not* the will of God that Alex die; that when the waves closed over the sinking car, God's heart was the first of all our hearts to break.[1]

Where was God when Alex drowned? Where was God on 9/11? Where was God when my husband's eye fell on that younger woman? Where was God when my daughter was conceived with a genetic disorder? Where was God when young boys in the Sudan were nearly starved and then gunned down? Where was God five minutes ago when I blanched in the face of my depression? Where was God, period?

We ask, "Why?" We ask, "Where?" Many people, with plenty of decent reasons, have decided the answer to *Why?* is "There just can't be a good enough answer." So for them the answer to *Where is God?* must be "Nowhere at all." No wonder critics of Christianity trash our faith, as we claim to believe in a God who is good, we pray to a God for help—but then, look what actually happens down here!

The First Heart to Break

William Sloane Coffin offered a reply to "Where was God?" "When the waves closed over the sinking car, God's heart was the first of all our hearts to break." Seems like a small consolation. And yet this grieving father told the truth, the only truth that makes sense given the way God—who is all love, who gives us a wide berth down here to move around and act freely, but who never stops loving us even more than fathers love their own sons—has arranged our world.

To say that God does not cause wrecks or cancer or the generally lousy condition of life on this planet is not to say God is not responsible—the way a corporate CEO might try to shield himself from ethical shenanigans at lower levels of the company. God is responsible. The questions are: What form does that responsibility take? What kind of responsibility does love normally assume? When God was young, how did God arrange to be responsible for us?

We are not marionettes. We have discretion over what, where, when, and how we drive. We are mortal. If we love, we know we will suffer loss. And when we do, we weep. Our hearts break. God is no less the image of God than we are. God loves. God weeps over every slight or unimaginably harrowing loss down here. God knew about the accident before Alex's father, or the police, or anybody else did. God was with Alex at every moment. "Where can I go from your spirit?" (Ps. 139:7). Our tears were God's tears before they were our own. Love is like that.

How do we know such a thing? In ancient times, God spoke, God revealed God's heart through Moses, Jeremiah, Hosea, the psalmists, Paul, and John, and their writings over all these centuries still pulsate with a God who is relentless about loving us, who is apparently more shattered than we are when things go badly.

We know God's heart because of Jesus. Jesus learned of the death of his friend Lazarus and—what did he do? The shortest verse in the Bible is the most pregnant with the fullness of God: "Jesus wept" (John 11:35). Jesus wept over Jerusalem, he had immense compassion when he saw the crowds, he pitied Peter and even wicked Pontius Pilate and the very soldiers who gambled for his garment while he was gasping for breath on the cross. They taunted him: "Come down and save yourself!" But he bore the suffering, he just hung there, like the center of gravity for all people anywhere who have ever suffered or will ever suffer pain, death, thirst, rejection, hopelessness. Instead of lashing out at the perpetrators of evil, Jesus loved. His heart broke. He died, the way you and I die, or worse.

In a way, this heartbreak is the price God pays for being one God. In ancient times, people believed there were many deities, some capricious and harmful, others benevolent and protective. When bad things happened in Babylon or the land of Canaan, people felt caught in the crossfire between warring gods. The idea of conflicting gods battling things out provided a convenient explanation for evil. But to believe in only one God raises questions about that God,[2] and we must reconcile a good God with suffering. Christianity's solution is that the good God takes evil and suffering on God's own self in the crucifixion of Jesus. Suffering happens; God doesn't cause it so much as God bears it, God's heart breaks, God grapples with all evil on the cross, and a victory is won on Easter, a victory not fully realized until the end of time.

Where was God on 9/11? People wondered how that could be God's will. Was it divine punishment on New York? No, clearly it

was not God's will, or we should give Osama bin Laden a medal
for doing holy work. But where was God? God was in the towers
as they fell; God was crushed, just as Jesus was crushed by the evil
machinations of history on the cross. Where is God? Jesus cries
out, "My God, my God, why have you forsaken me?" But notice:
he still calls God "my" God. God is not remote in the hour of suffering. God is there, as close as your next breath, or your last
breath. God feels the pain, as much and even more than we do.

Is this small consolation? I think it's powerful. When my wife
and I were first married, she would try to tell me some of her personal aches, her problems. I would leap in like a valiant knight, to
tell her why she shouldn't feel the way she was feeling, or to offer
a quick fix to whatever was out of kilter. After a few years, she
admitted that this annoyed her. She wanted me to listen, to know,
so she could be heard, and known. We call this "love." Love
doesn't fix everything. Love doesn't clamp off feelings and tell you
they need not be. Love takes the pain of the other person and
shares it, bears it, feels it. God does no less.

God does more, too. God does not merely wallow in the depths
of the dark hole with us. God powerfully lifts us out of that hole.
God helps us make sense of where we find ourselves. God provides
us with friends and fellow sufferers, and eventually compensates in
ridiculously fantastic ways for what we have undergone.

But for now, and when suffering first strikes, we focus on the
cross, on the heart of God. God does not manipulate our world
or our lives down here, but God is not absent. In fact, God is especially present in moments of suffering. We tend to think that if
suffering is here, I want to get away from here and get over there,
back toward God, where there should be no suffering. But if anything, if we are in a place of light and breezy comfort, we do not
sense God. We need to enter the place of suffering, to feel our own
pain, gather near to those who are in pain, whose hope seems dried
up, who are crying out, "My God, why have you forsaken me?"
And there we find God.

God showed himself most clearly, profoundly, and tenderly, not
in a lovely beachside resort where a tan Jesus sips a daiquiri com-
fortably with his friends. God showed himself on the cross, a grue-

some death for someone entirely too young. That *was* God's will! so that we would never face evil or suffering alone, so that we would take comfort in a God who did not remain aloof in heaven, but came down, bore the worst the world could dole out, endured that kind of pain and agony we all endure eventually.

But Why Didn't God Intervene?

What if we believe in the power of prayer? What if we believe God acts, that God answers our pleas? or that God can and should shield us from harm or get engaged in some way to stop or alleviate evil? When the one I love is the one killed, when it's my beloved who has cancer, I find myself asking, "Why?"—this time not, "Why do bad things happen?" but, "Why didn't God intervene?" When Jesus arrived in Bethany, he didn't merely weep; instead of leaving Lazarus in the tomb, he raised him up. Jesus calmed the storm. Jesus restored the leper's health. Miracles seemed to happen in Jesus' vicinity, and we may hear rumors of miracles still happening in our world today.

So, why didn't God act when I needed God? Is God just removed from everything, grieving for us, yes, but sufficiently impotent as to be a worthless deity? These questions, when we ask them, are cries in the dark, as we have said. We only dare answer when the crisis isn't immediate, when the wound isn't raw. Why doesn't God intervene? Why does God *let* bad things happen?

Why does anything at all happen? Sometimes we stumble into the mistaken idea that God intervenes in inexplicable, miraculous, dazzling ways—and these occasional interventions are the sum total of God's activity. But is God busy only when something startling, something that defies the laws of nature, occurs? Is life in the world as it typically unfolds just a neutral fact with no divine significance, so that in this truly secular place we scan the horizon to see if God will swoop in and do something?

We try to delve into explanations for why God dipped a finger into this world, when all along God was never outside the world looking in, deciding to act then but not now. God made everything, God devised the gravity keeping you in your seat, God concocted the air you're breathing. God never deserts what God has made. God is always involved in everything.

Centuries ago we chalked up much of what transpired—a clap of thunder, sickness, victory in battle—to direct, divine intervention. As knowledge grows, the category "miraculous" seems to shrink. But should it? Isn't the ordinary, a flower blooming or the beaming of the sun, a good gift from the hand of God? Isn't it the case that, from God's perspective, either everything is a miracle or nothing is a miracle? The world and all that transpires within it is of God, and that grand fact stirs in us what Martin Buber called "an abiding astonishment,"[3] a sense of wonder.

The most abiding astonishment is that God loves, and love never manipulates. God is involved, but God loves too much to control. If God reached down and yanked hard on a budding flower, the petals would be crushed. It seems to be God's will to let the sun shine and the rain fall. In joy and immense gratitude, the flower turns its face to the sky and blooms colorfully, stretching down into the dark soil to find a subtle drink of sustenance. If God reached down and "intervened" in the details of your life, blocking an accident here, rearranging your DNA there, violating another person's free will to prevent a crime, or snatching this person from a burning building but leaving another behind, the flower of humanity, the dream of love, would be crushed. It seems to be God's will to let the sun shine and rain fall, and we in joy and gratitude turn our faces to the sky and blossom, reaching down for the drink we crave.

So why was there no miracle for the one I loved? Part of the answer is that God chooses not to control all events down here. But what about an occasional "miracle"? Jesus did not merely glorify God for the created course of affairs and then leave people alone; he acted decisively, clearly "intervening."

Jesus' Miraculous Power

But we may notice a curious wrinkle in the stories of Jesus' miracles. He dazzled the disciples with his miraculous acts, but then told them to be rather hush-hush about it all, almost as if he sensed that the sheer exercise of miraculous power would be misconstrued, that people would pin their fantasies on him, that the unscrupulous would devise plans to capitalize on his wizardry.

More importantly, we notice that Jesus evidently performed whatever miracles he performed, not to impress anybody with his power, but to teach a lesson. And, at least as far as we know, he healed not in private, but in public, in front of a crowd, and he always attached a sermon; his miracles were designed to bring home a "point." He healed a blind man, and did so in front of the Pharisees, to demonstrate that they were the truly blind ones, blind to the dawning reign of God being advertised by Jesus' miraculous power.

Did Jesus care if the blind man regained sight? Yes. But every day in every place as Jesus traveled, many people stayed sick, limped, couldn't see, and died. He did not heal everyone. It does not seem to have been Jesus' desire for every person to be healthy and live long; he was selective, intervening only here or there, and apparently only when that intervention had the chance to make a stellar point that would have an impact on the masses.

Do inexplicable cures fit this model? Does God "cure" today, not just so the sick will feel better, but for some larger purpose? We do not know. I know an extraordinarily effective pastor who, as a young man, had little more than a casual interest in religion until his mother was diagnosed with an inoperable cancer that the doctors said would fell her in six months. But after six months, the cancer, whose only treatment was the prayers of friends and family, had vanished. Her son was catapulted by that experience into a phenomenal ministry to hundreds of people. Did God cure her so he would embrace his vocation? We hesitate to draw this conclusion, which could be right, could be wrong.

And as a pastor myself, in all candor, I prefer not to tell my friend's story. Yes, people are eager to hear stories of stunning cures. But I find that in my lifetime of ministry I have prayed for untold thousands of people, church members, kin of church members, friends, acquaintances. Out of all those, virtually all—I would estimate more than 99 percent—follow the expected course laid out by the diagnosing physician.

Yes, people facing laparoscopic gall bladder surgery solicit prayers, and they do well. But crooks and atheists with gall bladder woes recover nicely with no prayers at all. Show me an Alzheimer's case being reversed by prayers, or pancreatic cancer eradicated. Cures that have been pronounced as miraculous by Christian physicians I know well are exceedingly few—so few that I do not often speak of the three "miraculous" cures I've been associated with. After all, three in several thousand isn't a very optimistic number.

If Jesus healed, but healings didn't become a regular staple of the Christian life, then why did he heal anybody at all? The answer is the same as to the question, "Why did God come down to earth in Jesus?" His agenda wasn't health and physical well-being, but salvation. Miracles are signs of the salvation to come. Jürgen Moltmann put it well:

> *Healing* vanquishes illness and creates health. Yet it does not vanquish the power of death. But *salvation* in its full and completed form is the annihilation of the power of death and the raising of men and women to eternal life. In this wider sense of salvation . . . people are healed not through Jesus' miracles, but through Jesus' wounds; that is, they are gathered into the indestructible love of God.[4]

God does not sit back and refuse to remove cancer cells or block a car crash. Neither does God sow cancer cells in people's bodies or hurl automobiles into one another. God would not do that to a son or a daughter; or to a young husband or to the parents of one who dies. God sees our suffering—and instead of having nothing to do with it and washing his hands of it, God comes down and takes our suffering upon himself. God, instead of washing his hands, held out his hands, and they were bloodied not just with his pain but with our pain, with our loss, and with our anguish. God does not leave us alone. The world did the worst it could do to him, and they slammed him in a grave with a guard and a stone over it. But God did not leave him in the grave. God raised him up so that, no matter what horrors we endure, we never need to look at God and wonder, "Why did you do this terrible thing to me?"

We must learn how to deal with this better. The worst, the hardest, the most haunting funeral I ever had was one you may have seen on the news. ABC, CNN, all the local news channels: everyone showed up for the spectacle of the death of a small child, and the death was clearly the fault of the father. In a crazy moment of inexplicable negligence, he had caused the death of his own precious son he loved more than his own life. I have never seen so much sorrow up close.

We got through the service and then drove to the cemetery. After saying "Amen" to the closing prayer, I opened my eyes and saw a woman walking toward—me? No—toward the father, standing next to me. She had a huge, broad smile on her face—surely the only person within a dozen square miles with any reason to smile on this darkest of days. Why was she smiling? So holy, so pious, so spiritual, she looked at this father who had just buried his son, and said, "You should rejoice. God took your child. God needed your child more than you did." He very calmly looked at her and said, "I don't believe that."

We don't believe that. God loves us. God would not kill our children, or kidnap them to live far away from us. God bears our suffering. God comes to redeem the worst losses we might ever endure. God is not the doer of evil, but the God who redeems evil. If we could understand this good, loving, powerful God, we would notice suffering out there, and we would ask, "How can I be part of the answer to why there is suffering? What is the power I have within me to alleviate the ache, to do battle with evil?"

Questions for Discussion

1. Why is it important for us to realize that God is not remote in our hour of suffering and that "God feels the pain, as much and even more than we do"?
2. If you pray for something and no "miracle" occurs, does that disturb your faith in a loving God?
3. In what ways have you experienced God taking upon God's self your sufferings?

Chapter Eight

God's Will for Good

A nd there is more: God did not merely take our suffering into the body of his own Son. A God who merely sympathized with us, who got down into the lowest depths with us, would be a kindhearted God—but we need a powerful God, a God who can take those who suffer horribly and raise them up at the final resurrection, a God who can judge the powers of this world who unleash suffering, and even bend them to the eventual good of God's purpose.

What can we possibly mean by speaking of "God's purpose," if God is not the master controller? God's purpose assumes many forms in the face of suffering and evil. There seem to be lessons we can learn from bad things that happen. There seem to be possibilities to discover meaning even in the worst circumstances. And there seem to be virtually miraculous transformations when God not only plucks good out of the teeth of disaster, but actually uses what is evil to bring about good.

Good from Evil

Consider the story of Joseph (the son of Jacob, not the husband of Mary). With multiple spouses and bickering sons, Jacob's family is patently dysfunctional. Joseph is his father's favorite; and between his dreaming that his older brothers would bow down to him and

Jacob's gift of special clothes, Joseph draws the ire of his brothers. Plans to murder him are jettisoned so they can make money by selling him as a slave to the Ishmaelites. They tear his garment, bloody it, and plunge the ultimate dagger into their father's heart. What else could he conclude but that his beloved Joseph was dead?

But Joseph survives, rising from prison to a position of power in the courts of Pharaoh. He's got brains, courage, and some mix of God's blessing and sheer luck—which the brothers back home don't have. A famine compels them to go down to Egypt, the breadbasket of the world. In a stunning plot twist, the person they must ask for bread is their own brother, Joseph. Naturally, they don't recognize him; but he recognizes them. After dallying with them a bit, he dismisses his entourage from the room, lets loose long pent-up emotions, gathers himself, dries his tears, and reveals the secret: "I am Joseph, your brother."

The brothers must be stricken with shock, horror, guilt, trepidation, remorse. But how does Joseph deal with those who treated him and his father so cruelly? His words must have taken light years to sink in: "Do not be distressed, angry with yourselves, because you sold me here; for God sent me before you to preserve life" (Gen. 45:5). Even after the glorious reunion with his father, even after Jacob's death, Joseph says the most remarkable thing: "Do not be afraid! . . . As for you, you meant evil against me; but God meant it for good, to bring it about that many people should be kept alive" (Gen. 50:19–20 RSV). Joseph forgives; he casts their common life into the hands of God's intent.

Notice that the brothers aren't given a "second chance," another crack at getting it right. They never get it right, they never "make up for" what they have done. We cannot praise their new, improved attitude. Weatherhead once wrote that "there is an opportunity in suffering which it is God's will that we should take and turn to our own, and the world's, high advantage. . . . There is an alchemy which turns all things into spiritual gold, and that alchemy is the right attitude to them."[1]

But God does not depend on any attitude change among the brothers (or us), however helpful an improved attitude might be.

God quite simply uses the evil they perpetrated and transforms it into good. Not that God caused them to do evil: God did not make them sell their brother or break their father's heart. But God gathered up their misdeeds, the broken will of God, and pieced it all together for God's good purpose.

God can do this. God can bring good out of evil. Everything here depends on God, not us, or our attitude, or our capitalizing on a second chance. And how lovely is this for us? We trudge around like Atlas, feeling the weight of the world on our shoulders. No wonder we're exhausted. Our lives are littered with the debris of our mistakes, the carnage of our guilt. But our hope is that God can overcome all that is evil—and that God can even use our mistakes, and somehow in the long run bring us and our world to God's own good end, which cannot be thwarted.

Maybe our lives are patterned like a beautiful Persian rug. Up close, this curve or that shape seems to be just some dark, ugly thread. But woven around and through are surprising, recurring threads of beauty, with the finished work a fascinating thing of joy. God doesn't cause evil; but God can manage it, reshape it, and bring good out of it all. As Hemingway put it in *Farewell to Arms*, "The world breaks everyone and afterward many are strong at the broken places."

Examples abound. A young man dies in a car accident, but through organ donation someone else lives on. A middle-aged woman battles breast cancer nobly, and her surviving friends and family are bolstered in their faith because of her stellar faith. Wounds are indelibly etched in the soul of one who grew up in a broken home, but as an adult she becomes a great artist whose work speaks to many who are themselves broken. Coping with job loss or illness, a family discovers for the first time the depth of love that unites them. The witness of martyrs buoyed the vitality of the Church.

And consider the lingering effects, the residual aftermath of pain: I love the insight Graham Greene shared in *The End of the Affair*. A woman notices what used to be a wound on her lover's shoulder, and contemplates the advancing wrinkles in his face:

I thought of lines life had put on his face, as personal as a line of writing—I thought of a scar on his shoulder that wouldn't have been there if once he hadn't tried to protect another man from a falling wall. The scar was part of his character, and I knew I wanted that scar to exist through all eternity.[2]

The scars in Jesus' hands and side were not blotted out by the resurrection. And thinking of the way "the world breaks everyone": I know that, for me, if I have any giftedness that matters to anybody else, it is not because of strength of body or native mental brilliance that I am able to be of help. I find my calling and my best contribution to the world in the place in me that has been wounded, in my weakness, in my vulnerability.

A host of Christians could tenderly counsel us, saying, "If you want to do God's will, look into that inner place where you have been hurt, where you carry some hidden ache, and there you will find God, and the transforming power of God to use you." My daily prayer while my children were young was "Lord, help me to be the best parent I can be, but then use my inevitable mistakes to bring them good in spite of me."

Even in the hour of death, our own or that of someone we love, we find God's tender action to bring good out of evil, especially as we remember that our ultimate destiny is not a life forever preserved on this earth. Thomas Merton's father died after a ferocious bout with cancer. Listen to the way Merton speaks of the suffering, not attributing the cancer or pain to God, but finding God's sure labor in the thick of it all:

> Behind the walls of [my father's] isolation, his intelligence and his will . . . were turned to God, and communed with God Who was with him and in him, and Who gave him, as I believe, light to understand and to make use of his suffering for his own good, and to perfect his soul. It was a great soul . . . and this affliction, this terrible and frightening illness which was relentlessly pressing him down even into the jaws of the tomb, was not destroying him after all. Souls are like athletes, that need opponents worthy of them . . . My father

was in a fight with this tumor, and none of us understood the battle. We thought he was done for, but it was making him great. And I think God was already weighing out to him the weight of reality that was to be his reward . . . and his struggle was authentic, and not wasted or lost or thrown away.[3]

The Lord Disciplines

There are lessons we learn only in the cauldron of suffering. C. S. Lewis, perhaps the past century's most popular writer on this subject, imagined God speaking to us like this:

> Whatever suffering it may cost you in your earthly life, whatever inconceivable purification it may cost you after death, whatever it costs Me, I will never rest, nor let you rest, until you are literally perfect.[4]

How do we think about God teaching us, perfecting us through suffering—especially if we do not think of God as the one who inflicts suffering upon us?

> The Lord disciplines him whom he loves . . . We have had earthly fathers . . . who disciplined us for a short time at their pleasure, but God disciplines us for our good, that we may share his holiness. For the moment all discipline seems painful rather than pleasant; later it yields the peaceful fruit of righteousness to those who have been trained by it. (Heb. 12:6–11 RSV)

Does the Lord discipline? What is discipline? The word "discipline" has fallen on hard times, having been reduced to the sour connotation of punishment or retaliation. I annoyed my seventh-grade science teacher by hurling spitballs that latched onto the ceiling. Even though I pleaded my intent was to fashion a solar system, a big yellow spitball for the sun, something much smaller and darker for Neptune, and so forth, she yanked me by the ear, hauled me out of the room, and laid into my backside with a wooden paddle with holes bored in it to exacerbate the pain. Does God "discipline" in this way? We sin, and then God, at the end of the divine rope, has had enough? To teach us a lesson, God causes a fender bender, a tornado, or a rapidly spreading influenza?

Perhaps we can think about God's discipline in a more helpful, less ferocious way. God acts, God does teach and discipline. But it's not revenge, it's not even punishment. It's all educative, designed to make us better. The God of love isn't petty; God wants only good for us. God is the good teacher, not the stern reprimander.

And perhaps there is an indirection about the way this discipline unfolds. Consider the way we conceive of God's blessings. We may pray, just as we have sat down to the family dinner table, thanking God for the food. We do not mean, for one moment, that God floated a prepared plate of meatloaf, rice, and broccoli, with garnish, down out of heaven, plopping it onto the table before us. We give thanks to God, if we think about it, for the complex, broader set of circumstances that put this plate of food before us: for God's creation of an earth that yields things that grow and are edible, for the rain, for the labor of farmers in another state, for those who harvest, process, and package, for the one who stocks the grocery shelves, the guy who asks, "Paper or plastic?" and the wonder of refrigeration, for the people and factors that led to our having sufficient funds to buy the food, for the one we know and love who labored in the kitchen. We remember those on whom we are dependent, whom we normally take for granted, and we also remember those who have no one to cook, don't have the money for food, or live in places where it hasn't rained enough to produce any bread. We thank God, and we fully understand the indirection, the way God provides a chain of events, and we also notice our responsibility with respect to others. God is great, God is good—so let us thank God for our food.

Isn't God's "discipline" like that? God creates the world in a way that, if we live in sync with God, there is a smoothness, a goodness fulfilled. If we cut against the grain, if we step out of bounds, there are lessons to be learned.

When my daughter was three, she teetered near the kitchen stove. I warned her several times to stay away, that the surface was hot—but she eventually planted her palm on the searing red-hot eye, and she screamed as her hand was ribboned with blisters. Did I press her hand against the eye to teach her a lesson? Did I sternly upbraid her and say, "See, I told you so"? No, I swept her into my arms, I held her, I applied medicine and cool cloths, and over many days nursed her hand back to health. Isn't God's discipline at least as good as mine?

Children, as they grow up, need much love and much structure. God provides a structured universe in which we grow as God's people. To flout that structure, to ignore the wisdom of the Creator, to flail beyond our God-given limits, is to court disaster, to invite lessons. "The Lord disciplines those whom he loves."

Perhaps, then, we can think of the wrath of God in the same way. Many will object to our suggestion in chapter 1 that God does only what is good, that evil never is hurled from the hand of God. But what about all the biblical passages that speak of the wrath of God? Clearly in the Old Testament (and in the New!), biblical people saw suffering as divine retribution, punishment doled out against God's people. We need not be surprised: in the ancient world, every moment of life was regarded as hinged to God, who caused the sun to rise, who sent diseases no one understood or could treat, who indeed was passionate about holiness, who was perceived as acting directly and personally at all times. So when bad things happened, people wondered, "Why did God do that to me?"

Many theologians, perhaps most famously Martin Luther, have put their finger on the way Isaiah explained the wrath of God: "Alien is his work!" (Isa. 28:21). God's "proper" work is love, blessing, salvation; but when we position ourselves as rebels against God's proper work, when we hurl ourselves at right angles (wrong angles!) against God's proper direction, we feel the back side, the dark side of God—God's "alien" work. The indirection of it is no different from the way we think of the food on the table.

God does not grow angry with my indulgent, gluttonous lifestyle and then, in wrath, plague my body with a heart attack; but there are consequences, the alien side of God's good work, to consuming too much alcohol and fatty foods. God does not plant a hollowness in my soul because I didn't read my Bible enough;

but there is a very real result to living out of sync with God. If there is such a thing as the wrath of God, its holy intent is nothing other than our good, our healing, our salvation. Divine wrath is real, but isn't petty or reactionary. God is deadly serious about how we live, and there are dire consequences to living out of sync with God—but we need not imagine God lashing out as the explanation of bad things that transpire.

Good comes out of evil. But is this *always* true? Is suffering always transformed into some good? Are there always positive lessons to be learned? We cannot know for certain. Perhaps it's wisest to say yes, God brings good out of evil—but avoid adding "always." Some evils are so horrific that the enormity of the pain is trivialized if we blithely claim some good will come from it. Dorothee Soelle stated her theological perspective on the holocaust rather strongly: "No heaven can rectify Auschwitz."[5] Not only do we seem to flunk the test of the lessons of history; the course of human events is littered with so much awful debris we can never think up enough wise lessons to make sense of it all. And we dare not trivialize the death of one mother's child by meagerly declaring there is some lesson to be learned.

Signs of Hope

After suffering, we do thrash about, looking for something good. Your husband or daughter or best friend has died, and you find yourself wondering if he or she is somehow flitting about, if there is some sign of the loved one's eternal life with God or ongoing vigilant presence with you. Back in chapter 2, we exposed the "hunch" method that looks around for signs. When it comes to suffering, and to dealing with agonizing loss, the yearning for a sign is different—and God, in God's overflowing mercy, may provide us with a sign or two.

Years ago, I had a close friend named Clay, a gastroenterologist—and single. He stunned all of us when he adopted a little girl named Lauren. Clay proved to be a superb dad. The day came for Lauren's baptism, and it was lovely. Somewhat strangely, after the service, a woman who had never met Clay spoke to me: "I had a vision during that baptism: the roof of the building lifted off, and light streamed down on the child from heaven, and a host of angels from heaven gathered around the font." I thanked her and forgot about it.

For five years, that is. Late one night Clay (who had since moved to Texas) called to tell me he had been diagnosed with brain cancer and had only a few months to live. The prospect of losing my friend was compounded by the thought of Lauren, a kindergartner, losing her only parent. After a restless night, I was opening my mail the next day and found a notecard from the woman who'd had the vision at the baptism. She had thought about it again, commissioned an artist to paint her vision, and had the painting made into notecards—and thought I would like one.

I tried to do the math and calculate the odds of this woman's having this vision during this particular baptism, of her sticking the card in the mail on the very day Clay, whom she still had never met and who was now living hours away, learned of his diagnosis. Although I know skeptics could muster some explanation, the odds against this coincidence being random are astronomical. But what did it mean? Hesitantly I told a friend, whose face lighted up as he said, "He's going to be healed!" But Clay lasted only a few months, and I found myself on a plane to Texas to preach at his funeral.

After I arrived, I kept fumbling with my briefcase, knowing I had packed the notecard with the vision of the angels. Should I share the notecard? To withhold the evidence I held, no matter how foggy I might be about its meaning, would be to slam a window shut when we really needed some light. So I told those present about the vision, the card, and how it came in the mail. A jaw or two dropped, a few people nodded; one man rolled his eyes.

"I don't know what this means," I admitted, "but it has to mean something. Perhaps when Lauren was baptized, the dark shadow in Clay's head that would eventually lengthen and be his undoing was perceived by the God we invoke in worship. And perhaps God, who is never happy to leave such a shadow to become nothing but darkness, flashed a small light in another mind, so that we could see a small flicker, some intimation of grace bridging space and time so we might detect the goodness of God in the darkness."

Yes, our theology requires us to believe that in Baptism, both Lauren *and* Clay were sealed with the Spirit and claimed by a God whose power manifests itself in the liturgy and Scripture. But doesn't God's power also show itself in the minds and hearts of all kinds of folks and in the most surprising of places? Isn't grace sneaky like that, tiptoeing up behind us in the dark, making no sense whatsoever? Does Baptism ever make sense? Did Jesus' Baptism make sense to anybody standing by the Jordan that day long ago?

We understandably look for signs, and perhaps God gives one now and then. But God always gives the sign of the cross, the sign of water in Baptism, the sign of the body and blood of Christ, clear indicators of the grace of God, conveyors of the power of God, anticipating the glory God promises to us.

In Harold Kushner's famous book *When Bad Things Happen to Good People*, he suggests that bad things don't have meaning when they happen: "But we can give them a meaning. We can redeem these tragedies from senselessness by imposing meaning on them."[6] We may try valiantly to "impose" meaning. But meaning isn't our burden to bear. We need not impose meaning. God in God's grace supplies the meaning. Hope depends on God, not on us. We discover our solidarity with Christ, suffering with us, redeeming the time, and pointing us to God's future. There is a shimmering good promised to us. We may get a few glimpses in this life, but truth be told, the genuine good God gives isn't in this world at all.

Questions for Discussion

1. In what ways does God bring good out of evil?
2. Have you experienced the "discipline" of God in ways that help to educate you? When?
3. What "meaning" have you sensed in any of your life's sufferings?

Chapter Nine

When God's Will Is Done

A recurring theme in this book has been that, very often, God's will is not done. But at the end of the day, at the end of time, that nagging, haunting truth will be overturned. Yes, God's will wasn't done today; I tried to do God's will and maybe succeeded, but then I also failed today. But eventually, the will of God will be the order of the day, all day, every day. Now, in humility, we wait, we "mourn in lonely exile here . . . until the Son of God appear." In God's good time, the will of God will be done—perfectly, effortlessly, without exception—and then there will be no more rebellion or accidents or cancer or frustration. "Night shall be no more . . . for the Lord God will be their light" (Rev. 22:5 RSV).

We pray, "Thy will be done," and this is the one prayer we know (with utterly absolute certainty) will be perfectly answered. In the end, evil will be no more. "[God] will wipe every tear from their eyes. Death will be no more" (Rev. 21:4). All will be glory, everything will shimmer with holiness. Every person and the entire universe will mirror the brightness of God's glory.

But until then, in the meantime, there will be evil. The world will persist as a vale of tragedy, sin, and darkness in the thick of beauty, goodness, and wonder. David Bentley Hart said it best: "Until that final glory, the world remains divided. . . . Life and death grow up together and await the harvest. In such a world, our portion is charity, and our sustenance is faith."[1]

Charity—and faith. Charity: We love, we care, we anticipate that final glory to the degree we are able. When we pray, "Thy kingdom come, thy will be done, on earth as it is in heaven," we seek not just a future, but a presence in which I make up my mind that I will be about heaven down here on earth. If social class, race, or background mean nothing in heaven, they will mean nothing to me now. If tears are wiped away then, I will wipe a few away today. If anger and decadence will vanish in eternity, then I will be gentle and holy today. I will love—not merely because God wills me to love, but because God has loved me, and I recognize the other person as somebody God loves.

Faith: Belief is defined in Hebrews 11:1 as "the assurance of things hoped for, the conviction of things not seen." We live here today, but with our hearts already resident in God's future. We are invested, not in the things of this place, but in the dawning of God's eventual victory.

Yes, evil and suffering are having their day. But God allows them only so much time. Evil will eventually be banished. Evil will finally be the occasion for God's glory. Suffering will be the theater for God's grace. Easter, after all, happened in a cemetery, and as Jesus' tomb was transformed into a chorus of praise by the angels, so the entire universe will no longer be subject to decay and despair, but will be a magnificent opera of music, dance, grand costumes, and artistry extolling God, whose will most certainly will have been done.

While we wait, we pray—and I love the phrasing Thomas Cranmer wove into *The Book of Common Prayer*: "Keep in our minds a lively remembrance of that great day . . ."—the day at the end of all time. How fascinating! We remember a day that has not yet dawned. But we can remember, because it was promised long ago.

When we remember that day that is coming, we must be careful not to shortchange how truly marvelous it will be. Sometimes we trivialize eternal life. Heaven either sounds frightfully boring, or else is a glutton's delight: we eat bonbons or prize-winning barbecue all day, lounging by a pool, shooting a hole in one every time.

But heaven isn't so trivial. A while back I attended a funeral. I noticed a man I knew only a little on the front row, roughly my age, obviously the son of the woman being buried. I studied his face: a hardened jaw, a steely gaze, as if he had not smiled much in his life. No sign of grief, as some older, unspeakable pain or lack of love was etched in his face. Had his mother done this to him somehow? Did she and he share some common foe?

I shuddered to contemplate all the emotions and numbness . . . and then I got to daydreaming about what heaven will be, what it could be, what it had better be like. Fast-forward from that funeral to "when we've been there ten thousand years . . ." I see this man, this boy, his jaw receded a bit, his eyes lighter, the corners of his mouth turned up. His mother walks up behind him, and she laughs, and they hug. He has a few tears, but they are tears of joyful love.

Heaven isn't me basking forever in all that I have enjoyed here on earth. Heaven is healing, heaven is reconciliation. Nicholas Wolterstorff wrote the best book on grief I have ever read: *Lament for a Son*, reflections on the death of his twenty-three-year-old son, Eric. He asks:

> What do I do now with my regrets, the times I placed work ahead of being with him, the times I unreasonably got angry, the times I hurt him . . . the times he did something wonderful and I was oblivious? What do I do with my regrets? When a person is living we can make amends. I believe God forgives me. But the matter between Eric and me? What do I do with my God-forgiven regrets? I shall live with them, and I shall allow them to sharpen the vision and intensify the hope for that great day when we can all throw ourselves into each other's arms and say "I'm sorry." The God of love will surely grant us such a day. Love needs that.[2]

It will be God's will for us to reconcile, to make peace, to love fully, as God has loved us all along.

In her charming novel *Animal Dreams*, Barbara Kingsolver tells about the town of Grace, where every year they celebrate the "Day of the Dead." The citizens go out to the cemetery and decorate the tombs, strewing flowers all over the ground; they share a festive meal, children run and play and sing among the graves—all of this done with loving care. Kingsolver concluded: "It was a comfort to see this attention lavished on the dead. In these families you would never stop being loved."[3]

In heaven we will be fully known, and fully loved. Good thing, since on this earth, no matter how special we feel, we will be forgotten. There is a kind of oblivion into which we all will drift—and it starts way sooner than we care to admit. Move to another town for a few years, and then come back to visit old friends. Or attend a high school reunion. People are mildly happy to see you. But they have moved on, as you have moved on. We are drifting into oblivion.

You wanted to make your mark on the world, to do something memorable. But one day all memory of you will fade—and let me suggest that this is not a bad thing. My high school chorus had maybe a hundred singers, and two of us—two!—were boys. The pressure on my fragile teen ego was ferocious; if I could only be a linebacker instead of one of two boys in the chorus. . . .

But then Mrs. Griffin put us on a bus for some massed choir event down in Georgia someplace. I found myself now as just one of maybe a thousand singers, hundreds and hundreds of boys, a wonderfully charismatic conductor, a huge pipe organ. When we began to sing, the music was like a mighty tumult. I could have fallen off the risers or simply kept my mouth shut, and no one would have noticed. But I sang more lustily than I ever had, thrilling to my place among such a glorious flood of song. We sang an old spiritual: "Soon ah will be done a-wid de troubles ob de world. . . ." A thousand voices singing softly, an undercurrent pulsating, tremendous energy—and then the men thundered together: "Goin' home to live wid God! . . . I want to meet my Jesus. . . ."

Soon we will be done with the troubles of the world. We're going home to live with God. We are drifting toward oblivion, toward being "lost in wonder, love, and praise." Those we have loved, and we ourselves, will be forgotten—perhaps the way an individual grape, or a single grain of wheat, drifts into the oblivion of a cask of wine or a loaf of bread, and on the table together become the body and blood of our Lord.

Or the way a small drop of water, a tear, or the mist, joins an innumerable host of other droplets of water, and I become part of a cloud, just a drop in a cloud of witnesses, and it is at the very end of the day, as the sun returns to its resting place, that the drops, the cloud, refracts the light of the sun and multiplies itself into stunning hues, a dazzling dance of stunning color, the glory of God Almighty, the beauty we know only as darkness descends.

But the color won't blind us. We will see, perhaps for the first time. The chorus will surge, and then the song will break up into what could only be described as laughter, the kind that elicits knowing looks among those who get it; tears will flow down our faces and join the river that makes glad the city of God. We see each other, and we love, not only each other and those who have, like us, failed so miserably to get God's will done, and we will turn together, the laughter subsiding, a mighty multitude in stunned silence before the God who for so long has wanted us to seek and understand the divine will, the divine desire, the heart of the one true God who never let us drift very far from the very will of God that mystified us. And in that silence, when we are still, and finally at rest, we will see, hear, feel, touch, know, understand, and embody the will of God. Now we pray, "Thy will be done," and when God's will is finally realized, our joy will be unspeakable.

Questions for Discussion

1. What is your vision of "heaven," where God's will is "the order of the day, all day, every day"?
2. In what ways does believing that God's will ultimately will be done bring comfort and hope?
3. If eternal life means reconciliation and peace and love as expressions of God's will then what are the implications for our lives here and now?

Notes

Introduction

1. Elie Wiesel, *Night*, trans. Marion Wiesel (New York: Hill & Wang, 2006), 34.

Chapter One: The God Who Wills

1. Robert Coles, *Dorothy Day: A Radical Devotion* (Reading, MA: Addison-Wesley, 1987), 16.
2. Stephen B. Oates, *With Malice toward None: The Life of Abraham Lincoln* (New York: Penguin, 1978), 446.
3. John Hick, *Evil and the God of Love* (Glasgow: Collins, 1966), 295.
4. Jon M. Sweeney, *The St. Francis Prayer Book: A Guide to Deepen Your Spiritual Life* (Brewster, MA: Paraclete, 2004), 125–26.

Chapter Two: God's Will for Me

1. Bruce K. Waltke, *Finding the Will of God: A Pagan Notion?* (Grand Rapids: Eerdmans, 1995), 17.
2. Leslie Weatherhead, *The Will of God* (Nashville: Abingdon, 1944), 42.
3. Samuel Wells, *Improvisation: The Drama of Christian Ethics* (Grand Rapids: Brazos, 2004).
4. Ibid., 12.
5. St. Francis de Sales, *Finding God's Will for You*, trans. John K. Ryan (Manchester, NH: Sophia Institute, 1998), 52–53.
6. Mother Teresa, *A Simple Path* (New York: Ballantine, 1995), 99.
7. Weatherhead, *The Will of God*, 46.
8. Maggie Ross, *The Fountain and the Furnace* (New York: Paulist, 1986), 80.
9. Patricia Loring, *Spiritual Discernment: The Context and Goal of Clearness Committees* (Wallingford, PA: Pendle Hill, 1992).

103

Chapter Three: God's Will Undone

1. Martin Luther King Jr., *A Testament of Hope: The Essential Writings and Speeches of Martin Luther King Jr.*, ed. James Melvin Washington (San Francisco: HarperCollins, 1986), 225.
2. Henry Blackaby and Claude King, *Experiencing God: Knowing and Doing the Will of God* (Nashville: LifeWay, 1990), 116.
3. Thomas Merton, *Thoughts in Solitude* (New York: Noonday, 1956), 83.
4. For more on Francis and the will of God, see my *Conversations with St. Francis* (Nashville: Abingdon, 2008), chap. 1.

Chapter Four: God's Will for Us

1. Charles Marsh, *Wayward Christian Soldiers: Freeing the Gospel from Political Captivity* (New York: Oxford Univ. Press, 2007), 16.
2. Ibid., 72, 46.

Chapter Five: When Bad Things Happen

1. Amy Tan, *The Kitchen God's Wife* (New York: Ivy, 1991), 26–27.
2. David Burrell, *Deconstructing Theodicy: Why Job Has Nothing to Say to the Puzzled Suffering* (Grand Rapids: Brazos, 2008).
3. C. S. Lewis, *The Problem of Pain* (London: Macmillan, 1940), 81. In the film *Shadowlands*, Lewis (played by Anthony Hopkins) vividly pounded his fist into his other palm as he spoke of God's hammer blows.
4. C. S. Lewis, *A Grief Observed* (New York: Bantam, 1976), 1.
5. George Eliot, *Adam Bede* (New York: Signet, 1961), 198.

Chapter Six: Why Bad Things Happen

1. Rick Warren, *The Purpose Driven Life* (Grand Rapids: Zondervan, 2002), 22–23.
2. David Bentley Hart, *The Doors of the Sea: Where Was God in the Tsunami?* (Grand Rapids: Eerdmans, 2005), 49–50.
3. Alan Jacobs, *The Narnian: The Life and Imagination of C.S. Lewis* (San Francisco: HarperSanFrancisco, 2005), 278–79.
4. C. S. Lewis, *The Four Loves* (New York: Harcourt, Brace, 1960), 169.
5. Karl Barth, *Church Dogmatics*, vol. III, part 3, trans. G.W. Bromiley and R. J. Ehrlich (Edinburgh: T. & T. Clark, 1960), 295–96.

Chapter Seven: Where Is God?

1. William Sloane Coffin, "Alex's Death," *The Courage to Love* (New York: Harper & Row, 1982).
2. James Crenshaw argues that "the move away from many gods to a single deity came at a high price," in *Defending God: Biblical Responses to the Problem of Evil* (New York: Oxford Univ. Press, 2005), 54.

3. Martin Buber, *Moses* (Amherst, MA: Humanity, 1988), 75, explored in depth by Walter Brueggemann, *Abiding Astonishment: Psalms, Modernity, and the Making of History* (Louisville, KY: Westminster John Knox, 1991).

4. Jürgen Moltmann, *The Way of Jesus Christ: Christology in Messianic Dimensions*, trans. Margaret Kohl (Minneapolis: Fortress, 1993), 108–9.

Chapter Eight: God's Will for Good

1. Leslie Weatherhead, *Salute to a Sufferer* (Nashville: Abingdon Press, 1962), 89.

2. Graham Greene, *The End of the Affair* (New York: Penguin, 1962), 110.

3. Thomas Merton, *The Seven Storey Mountain* (New York: Harcourt, Brace, 1948), 83.

4. C. S. Lewis, *Mere Christianity* (New York: Macmillan, 1960), 172.

5. Dorothee Soelle, *Suffering*, trans. Everett R. Kalin (Philadelphia: Fortress, 1975), 149.

6. Harold Kushner, *When Bad Things Happen to Good People* (New York: Avon, 1983), 136.

Chapter Nine: When God's Will Is Done

1. David Bentley Hart, *The Doors of the Sea: Where Was God in the Tsunami?* (Grand Rapids: Eerdmans, 2005), 103.

2. Nicholas Wolterstorff, *Lament for a Son* (Grand Rapids: Eerdmans, 1987), 64–65.

3. Barbara Kingsolver, *Animal Dreams* (New York: HarperCollins, 1990), 163.